Keep Your Hands Out of My Pocket

Keep Your Hands Out of My Pocket

◆

Strategies to Get More for Your Money

Robert E. Tevis

iUniverse, Inc.

New York Lincoln Shanghai

Keep Your Hands Out of My Pocket
Strategies to Get More for Your Money

iUniverse, Inc.

For information address:
iUniverse, Inc.
2021 Pine Lake Road, Suite 100
Lincoln, NE 68512
www.iuniverse.com

ISBN: 0-595-28300-4 (pbk)
ISBN: 0-595-65756-7 (cloth)

Printed in the United States of America

This book is dedicated to my parents who worked hard for my education and to my wife who inspires me to use my education every day.

Contents

1

Keep Your Hands Out of My Pocket

Do you ever get the feeling that everyone's after your money? It's true.

People involved in sales are constantly looking for ways to separate you from your hard earned cash. Sellers of high-priced goods and services are constantly receiving training from their on-the-job experience, as well as books and formal classes, on ways to trade their offerings for your cash or credit. Great salespeople are able to just reach right into your pocket and take all that you have to give.

Sometimes, they reach in with the subtlety of a pickpocket. You happily drive your new car away blissfully unaware that the dealer has taken you for a few thousand dollars more than you really had to pay. Imagine if you could have the car and keep the few thousand dollars for yourself. If you bought it on credit, imagine a lower monthly payment.

Don't get me wrong. These people are not out to rob you. They just want to get as much as they can for their product and service. They are people, just like you, who are trying to earn whatever they can to support themselves and their families. In fact, you might be in a sales profession yourself. This is nothing to be ashamed of.

In fact, salespeople are an integral part of the engine that drives our economy. I have worked for almost 25 years with salespeople in some of the top Fortune 500 companies. I have participated in sales training where some of the best salespeople in the technology business are trained to answer their customer's objections. This is another way of saying "you must continue selling, even if your customer's first response is no." It's their job to sell and earn what they can from a buyer.

Regardless of your profession, at one time or another, you also function as a buyer. The seller forms only the first half of the equation we call a free market. The other half is the buyer. A free market needs both a seller and a buyer who can freely act on their own behalf to transact a deal.

Buyers, however, often forget their responsibility to the free market, and act on behalf of the seller. They do this every time they buy something without question. Without buyers, acting on their own behalf, sellers can dictate the price and demand whatever they want. A good buyer performs a valued service in the marketplace by keeping prices for good ands services within reason.

Buyers, who routinely buy cars for $20,000, may see the price of cars slowly creep up towards $30,000; but buyers who stop buying at $30,000 will definitely see prices move downward toward $20,000. This is how buyers, interact with sellers, to make the modern marketplace work. This is the ebb and flow of the market.

The market is also helped by buyers who save some money from a single purchase and now have more money to spend somewhere else. In fact, you don't need a lesson in economics to know that it's good to save money on everything you buy. The adrenaline rush you get from keeping the money in your pocket will tell you all you need to know. The question is how you can win at a game that is clearly tilted in our society toward the seller.

The answer is that you need to develop your ability to negotiate. No one is born with this skill, but everyone can learn it. This book will give you the simple concepts you need to help you keep a lock on your pocket. It's your money. You should have the skills and knowledge to hold onto it as long as you can.

If you are like most people, you probably never gave a thought to learning how to negotiate. Most negotiation books are written for the sellers. Negotiation experts sell their experience to the people involved in sales or other business professions. After all, this is how the greatest salespeople in the world become great salespeople—they become great negotiators. Top sellers need to convince buyers that they have the absolute best product at the absolute best price.

To remain on top, professionals understand that they need continuous education and training. Most buyers never become professional at buying. They remain amateurs. They do not take the time to learn and practice what they learned. Unfortunately in the marketplace, buyers pay for this all the time. It's unfair that professionals receive this training and the amateurs, the buyers, learn nothing about it. If sellers have great tools to use to get you to buy something, buyers should also take a moment to get some great tools to even the score.

You would think that since you are destined to spend a huge portion of your life buying things, that teachers would have added negotiation skills to the reading, 'riting, and 'rithmetic lessons. Unfortunately, basic education has left out negotiation training.

I learned that you need to reach out and get this training on your own. I read the books and listened to the tapes. The major companies I worked for were kind enough to send me to live lectures with some of the best teachers in the area of negotiation skills. My MBA provided me with additional lessons, but you soon reach a point where you have to put all this knowledge to work.

As a manager in a large international company, I often had to pick up the phone, contact an employee who I never met, and convince that person to drop whatever he or she was doing and do something for me. That person could be in a foreign country, thousands of miles away. I had only a few seconds to introduce myself and convince the stranger that I needed help to get the job done. I always got the help I needed. While it is obvious that good communication skills were helpful, the negotiation skills I developed were essential to get the job done.

Most importantly, the same skills that I would use in my job, the same ones that I would share with our salespeople when I would consult with them, also worked extremely well in my personal life. They helped me get my home, my car, and most of the significant purchases I made. I simply applied the knowledge of how to negotiate to my everyday life. I proved to myself that good negotiation skills do pay off.

In fact, my wife constantly gets requests for my time to help someone we know go shopping. While I'm glad to help, the most rewarding times are when I am able to teach my friends and family how to use these concepts themselves. Anyone can learn to negotiate and get what they want for less.

About a year ago, an old tree was threatening to fall on my mother's property. Insects and disease had taken its toll on the tall, decades old oak. Like most people, my mom called a local tree service to have the tree taken down. She called to tell me that she was disgusted at what it costs to remove an old tree. When I found out I was disgusted as well.

The tree service wanted $4500.00. To me this was a lot of money. To my parents, living on a pension, this was obscene. "That's what it costs." My mother sighed. "No, Mom," I countered, "That's what the XYZ service wants."

There is a subtle, but very important difference between our comments.

My mother, inexperienced in buying such services, took the quote offered by the seller as "the price." Obviously, the XYZ tree service was in the business to cut down trees. The old, 60 foot tall oak was leaning precariously and threatening a nearby house. They told her it was a big job, and that they would require a lot of expensive equipment to get it done. Their detailed explanation made it sound reasonable to her.

To me, the price was still obscene no matter how you tried to justify it. I explained to her that she needed to consider the price as only the "first" quote. I told her she needed to shop tree services. I knew then that I would have to help her learn how to shop and negotiate for a lower price. Thankfully, mom was willing to listen. After some coaching, she finally got the idea.

A few weeks later, the tree was removed by another tree service. The cost was $1,500. Both of us felt great that we were able to save the $3000. I was also happy that she learned how to shop for a better price—a skill that she can continue to use everyday. A skill you will learn also in the following pages.

A few years ago, a friend of mine pulled up in front of our house with his new Toyota. This friend had always had a tough time making ends meet. I knew that, although it wasn't the hottest looking car on the street, it was probably the hottest looking car to him. After many years of old, used car miseries, he finally got his first new car.

Admiring the car, I asked how much he paid for it. I staggered when I learned he paid the sticker price. Now I don't like to see my friends hurt. Without commenting on the scandal, I asked him why he didn't negotiate for a better price. He answered, "I hate to haggle." He was happy with his new car, confident he could live with the monthly payments. His happiness over owning the car completely blinded him to the atrocious total cost.

He was not the only happy one. I am very sure that the dealer was also happy with his windfall. Meanwhile, I felt bad that my friend had lost so much money on getting the car he wanted—money that he really couldn't afford to lose.

I use these two examples to illustrate that you are free to choose the path that you want. If you are happy to spend your hard earned money for something at whatever price the seller wants to charge, you will find that you have a lot of company. Most people either do not know how to negotiate or do not want to even try.

If on the other hand, you are willing to try a few of the techniques that follow, you will find that you can still get the things you want and save some money in the process.

I believe that the majority of people fail to negotiate because they don't believe they can. There is a lot of comfort in just getting the price and then paying it. It seems very easy. Few people recognize that comfort costs real money.

Sure, when it comes to staying at the Ritz or the Downtown Motel, one definitely is more comfortable than the other and the price tag shows it. While many people recognize that comfort costs money when going first class versus coach, they fail to see that the comfort they experience in buying something easily also costs real money. You can save this real money if you take a little more active approach in your purchase.

Your first application of negotiation techniques will require you to step outside your comfort zone, but I promise you that you will find many of these steps financially rewarding.

At first, you might trip up. You may fail, but sooner or later you will notice that these techniques do work. The first time you succeed you will feel like you won the Super Bowl even if you only save a few dollars. As you gain through practice, you will save even more. You will be ecstatic when the savings amount to thousands. On large purchases, like those for cars or houses, this is clearly in the realm of possibilities. I have even saved hundreds on purchases under a thousand dollars.

One day, you will realize that the whole process of saving money through negotiation is really not that difficult. In fact, it will become downright comfortable, but comfortable on less money.

2

Don't be Afraid to Negotiate

A growing trend in our society is to move away from negotiated purchases. Our society, bred on fast food, wants to increase the speed of everything—including purchases. Vendors want to post the price and have the buyer pay the posted price. Any time spent on the negotiation of a purchase increases the total transaction time. This reduces the amount of goods and services that a vendor can deliver within a specific amount of time, and thereby reduces the amount of money that can be made. When you are measuring the amount of people you can push through a drive-up window per hour, you don't want to stop to negotiate. Buyers, rushing though those drive ups, appreciate the concern as well.

For example, even the most serious negotiator would not want to stop the checkout line at the supermarket to bargain for a carton of milk. In fact, most people are impatient when the scanner has trouble finding the bar code on the item. For a carton of milk, most buyers are willing pass up the savings they might have negotiated due to the increased convenience in the transaction.

Like the two edges to every sword, however, convenience cuts both ways. By saving the time you would lose to a negotiation, you also lose on your ability to save on a purchase. Improved convenience is one of the best techniques a seller has in removing the negotiability of his pricing. As people get more and more impatient in their purchases, sellers use this impatience to get the price they want for the product they are selling. They also lose the annoyance of having to haggle with you.

Even expert level negotiators, car dealers for instance, have responded to this trend with the growth of "no hassle" selling. For years they have wanted to sell their cars for their sticker prices. Now, under the guise of making the purchase of a car "easier" for you, they get people to part with thousands of dollars more than they would have if they just put up with the hassle. Who really gets the benefit from "no hassle" car purchases? Just look in your pocket and make a guess.

I wince every time I hear that someone paid the sticker price for a car. It takes me all my strength to smile and keep my mouth shut when someone tells me that this time it was different. This time they had to pay more because the dealer does not negotiate on, for instance, a particular luxury car. This just tells me that some people who are buying a high priced model are happy to pay more than they have too just to show that they can do it. I would rather they contribute the money they could save to a real charity. Again, convenience gets the nod. People have learned to pay for the right to avoid a negotiation.

Sadly, more than convenience is involved when you run into these people. Even when financial considerations have a significant impact on the person's ability to buy a simple car, people will shy away from negotiating. Answers like "I didn't want to bother." often disguise a more fundamental and serious issue. The most devastating reason of all for not negotiating is that you are simply afraid to negotiate.

Fear can be both the friend and the enemy of the successful negotiator. In most cases, if you are the one that is afraid, fear is definitely the enemy. Most sellers use fear to their advantage, and if they see it in you, they will find some way to use it.

Here are some examples of how sellers use fear that may seem innocuous, but are truly insidious when it comes to your ends. Think about the times when you hear the following phrases:

1. The sale ends today!

2. I can only hold this price until tonight.

3. This is the last one.

4. You must call within the next five minutes.

Each simple phrase is designed to capitalize on your fear of not getting what they are selling.

Needless to say, you have to have some guts to begin a negotiation. Think of the image of Oliver Twist, in the Charles Dickens' book of the same name. Oliver was just an orphan in a workhouse, sitting for his meal with hundreds of other abandoned boys. Finishing the little food that he was given, he strode up to the headmaster and said, "Please, Sir, I want some more."

If you have never read the Dickens' classic, you can see the critical scene played well by Mark Lester in the 1968 film "Oliver!"

Oliver Twist best illustrates the basic beginning to any negotiation. Always, politely ask for more than you are offered. After all, if you already had all that you wanted, there would be no need to negotiate.

If you remember the scene clearly, Oliver didn't stride up confidently and holler his demand. His approach was timid. In fact, Dickens writes that he was "somewhat alarmed at his own temerity." Afraid as he was, he had guts. He got up and asked for more.

Just think of what was going through his head as the master said "'What?' At length and in a faint voice."

He must have been terrified as he aroused the wrath in what was clearly and beyond doubt a major figure of authority in his life. He could have just let the headmaster's reaction put him down. He could have just walked back to his seat with his empty bowl.

But I would want to have such a gutsy negotiator on my side. Oliver's response was to ask again.

This time the headmaster's response was clear and instantly calculated to stop a possible run on him by the rest of the boys in the workhouse.

"The master aimed a blow at Oliver's head with a ladle; pinioned him in his arms, and shrieked aloud for the beadle." After which, the school board met and ordered the boy into instant confinement.

Now we find the reason that most people do not ask for more. At best, they might be rebuked and embarrassed and, at worst, someone might strike them in the head. Rarely, does the realization arise that there is a third outcome. They might just get more.

Let's take a closer look at the fear-inducing options that stop someone from going for the third successful option.

Here is an experiment to see what happens when you open yourself up to being rebuked and embarrassed

Go to a car dealer, find a car that has a sticker price of, let's say, $25,000. When a dealer walks up to you (Someone will. It is in their blood.) just say that you were looking for a car like this but cannot pay more than $20,000. See what happens. Unless there are some fantastic rebates on it, chances are that he won't be as constrained as the head-master in his verbal response. He might even laugh at you.

The fear is now welling up in you. Even if you are shaking, take a breath and then calmly and politely, ask again if he can sell this car for about $20,000.

The verbal abuse might increase but few car dealers would progress to anything physical, so you don't have to worry about the ladle in the head. One of two things is now going to happen.

If he is new in the game, he might walk away and write you off as an idiot. Unless you see this car dealer in your social circle, you have left one person roaming somewhere in the world who thinks you are an idiot. Unless your self-esteem is that fragile, you haven't lost anything. Most people are unlikely to take out a full page ad or give an interview to the New York Times about your idiocy. They feel better just getting away from you. If you want to avoid the bad publicity, just make sure they do not know your name before you try this.

On the other hand, he might just say something like this:

"You cannot possible buy this car for $20,000. We cannot sell this car for less than $22,000."

What was that? $22,000. Notice that clearly. Every dealer in America would gladly sell you a car for its posted price. Why would he drop his price? Well, we will cover that in the next chapter.

In the meantime, let's just focus on the "more" factor and the score.

Rebuked and Embarrassed: 1
Head wounds: 0
Potential savings: $3,000.

The question you have to ask yourself is very simple. If you could reduce your risk to nothing more than a rebuke or embarrassment, would you take that risk to save $3,000 on this car? A few hundred dollars on that camera? Or any amount of money on something that you really want.

Obviously if the danger of a head wound is present, you might reconsider. You would never want to put yourself in a position like Oliver, where asking could cause you some critical injury. Fear of true danger is a helpful characteristic of human beings. It keeps people out of the lion's mouth or some other dangerous place. However, sellers know that fear of embarrassment will also keep you from asking for a cheaper price and they will use it to manipulate you.

I have a friend in technology sales who always tells people, when he is in a disconcerting position, that he can't be embarrassed because he is in sales. He knows how this fear is used to manipulate his buyers, and he also knows it will not work on him because of his knowledge.

The solution is simple. Do not be afraid to ask or negotiate. Unless you are in some dangerous position, the only thing you risk is embarrassment. This is something you can get over as you count the money you save.

3

Assume People Are Ready to Bargain

You should always assume that a seller will negotiate with you. This concept may seem strange in a world where everything, from a can of peas to a house, has a posted price tag. This is just the seller's way of saying what he wants for the item. If you want to save money, or get more for our money, you are going to have to recognize that there is a difference between what the seller wants and what you really have to pay. We will review this concept in detail in the next chapter. For now, assume that every one will be ready to negotiate with you.

There are, though, some places where your ability to negotiate is limited or restricted. You can use some basic common sense to identify those places where you might not want to try a negotiation strategy. The drive up window and the supermarket are two places where, we have already seen, negotiation strategies are not going to work.

As the price rises on a particular good or service, however, negotiation becomes a more viable and necessary technique to use when transacting a deal. Eventually, you arrive at a point where, when dealing with valuable goods and services, negotiation is the only way people expect you to do business. This is a key point which we will explore later in this chapter.

In the meantime, let's just assume that the product or service you want to buy is one that gives you some room to negotiate. It doesn't matter if it is a new sofa, a car, or even a service. The basic reasons people will negotiate with you remain the same. Here are some of the most important reasons they are ready to bargain.

They need to sell a service to survive

People in service businesses live off of their ability to sell their service. They also live off of the basic idea of supply and demand. When demand for their service is great, they can demand from their customer whatever they want for their service. When demand is light, their customers can often dictate what they want to pay. The world of supply works here as well. If there are a hundred plumbers fighting over twenty jobs, pricing tends to go down. Conversely, if there are three in your town where 20 jobs exist, be prepared to pay and wait for help.

The rules of supply and demand also impact your ability to negotiate effectively. For example, let's say you need to hire someone to mow your lawn. If there are only three landscapers in your town, and their work is in great demand, and if many people are willing to pay their price, then they might not be willing to negotiate with you. The operative word here is "might."

If the service you require can be done by them quickly or easily, they might be willing to negotiate a lower price. In addition, business conditions change all the time. If the landscaper you chose has some slack in his business, or if he has some extra staff waiting for a project, he might be willing to negotiate.

For example, if he is paying a helper and he has no work for that person at that time, he might be willing to negotiate to improve his return on the cost of the helper.

In addition, if overall business conditions are down, he would probably be highly receptive to take on some additional work at a price lower than his going rate. In fact, there might really be more than three people who can get the job done.

How do you know if any of these possibilities exist? How can you find out if he can afford to do it for less? How do you uncover other ways of getting it done?

The answer is simple. You need to do some basic market research. You need to look around and find out the real market conditions for landscapers. Talk to some people who are using landscapers in our neighborhood. Look in the newspaper. Perhaps, if all you need is someone to mow the lawn, you could just put a flier in the local high school, or ask a neighbor if he knows someone who is mowing lawns in the neighborhood.

The reference desk at the local library is often one of the most over-looked resources for conducting local market research. These people are paid with your tax dollars to research questions for those who use the library. No question is too complex or too easy. People are some-times afraid to ask these blessed helpers something simple like "Do you know a cheaper way to get this particular service?" I know for a fact that these underutilized research assistants would be happy to solve a problem like this for you. Give them a chance.

Obviously, if we are talking about a service that amounts to a sizable amount of money, you need to allocate some time to do this research. The library is a good place to start when researching neighborhood issues. The internet also offers some valuable research tools. In fact, if you do not have your own internet connection, the library is the place to get connected.

If you don't have the time to do your own research or if the service does not concern a lot of money, you can conduct some basic research by asking the seller some questions. Don't be afraid. Just try this little dialog.

You: How much do you charge to (insert service here)?
Seller: $XXX.00
You: That much!? (At this point your face should flinch and you should not utter a single additional word.)

If you are following the cadence of this dialog, it is now up to the seller to answer your flinch. If you follow this example <u>exactly</u> as I described, the seller is left with the following choices:

1. How much can this person spend? Maybe, if I lower my price a bit he'll reconsider.

You will be surprised how often a seller takes this choice. If his price falls so much as a dime, you now have a clear indication that the service is negotiable. How far you want to take the negotiation is up to you.

Make sure you don't take it to the point of hurting the seller. The seller is just as human as you are and has just as much right to win. We will look at this concept of supporting a win for the seller later in the book. You don't want the guy fixing the brakes on your car, for example, trying to figure out how to get you back for a punishing negotiation experience. Try to find some reasonable amount where both you are happy with your savings and the seller is happy to get the business.

The seller can also respond to your flinch this way:

2. This person does not understand what I do for that much money. I have to sell him on my services.

This is the course that most sellers will take. Give the person a chance. Let the seller have the opportunity to sell his services. You might find that he does more for the money than other similar sellers. This is first person research. **Think of your first approach with a seller as though you are conducting a survey instead of thinking that you are ready to contract for the service.**

Make notes on exactly what this particular seller is offering. This is useful information to aid you in your negotiation. For example, if they offer you three services, you might be able to negotiate for just the two you wanted. Furthermore, you might be able to alter the terms of the offer to effect the saving you want based upon these details. At the very least, you learn how the business operates. This can help you when you talk to others in the same business.

While your goal is likely to get the best for your money, there are other benefits that you may want from the service. For example, they may charge only $25 to mow your lawn, but charge you another $25 to clean up the cuttings. Know what the seller is offering. Know the entirety of the service before you sign any contract. You are only going to find that out by asking, and asking is the first step in doing any research.

Let's assume that you made it past the research and the sales talk. Here is another easy way to push the seller into a negotiation to lower the price for you.

When the seller has finished his sales pitch, just repeat what you said the last time with just the addition of one, single word—"but."

You: "but, that much?" (Say no more)

Now it's up to the seller. Most will go into an expanded sales talk. Some will just take the new opportunity to speak to offer a lower price. He is now negotiable as described above.

If you are dealing with a truly smart and experienced seller, he may try to negotiate by offering to reduce the size of his offering or take out parts of the offering to see if he can convince you of the value of the package. This is one good way the seller has to make the sale without reducing his typical selling price. This also helps his relationship with existing customers. For example, if one of his customers finds out you paid less, the seller can always point out that you got less for your price.

Of course there is another choice the seller can make.

3. This person cannot afford me. I will just say thank you and move on.

If the seller takes this choice, don't give up. Be polite and thank him for his time. Offer him some means to contact you if he decides later to lower his price. After you part, he might reconsider and give you a call.

Your attitude should be that this was the result <u>this time only</u>. Maybe tomorrow, next week or next month, he will be more receptive.

If you cannot afford to wait, you now have some good, basic information from him. Try one of his competitors. Go through the same basic questions above. You should not disclose to the new seller ANYTHING about your prior experience. Some people use the, "Well, Joe tells me that he can do it for $50" technique. They think that this shows that they are clever and that they know the seller's business. They expect the seller to respond with a cheaper offer.

In fact, you are just starting a fight that is unnecessary and potentially dangerous. If I were the seller, I would say, "Then let's call Joe." I'll bet you'll feel comfortable with that.

Why, as a seller, do I need to know that you are clever anyway? There is no way you are going to know my business by just talking to one of my competitors. I know that and you should also. Rather than try to look clever, you can gain more by trying to look ignorant. After all if I, as a seller, feel sorry for you, I might do more for you. I will have little empathy for you if I feel that you are trying to put something over on me with your cleverness.

Remember, you are not buying yet, you are just DOING A SURVEY. Treat each seller as a new experience. Each one gives you the chance of learning exactly what each offers and how each is different. It is all right to ask questions based upon your research, but you should NEVER assume that you know the answer. Give the seller a chance to answer the question. You may find that you really did not know the answer after all. This is the learning part of the purchase process, and it is time well spent.

Some people will even ask the seller what his competitor charges. Some sellers can get downright angry at such a question. I was once verbally abused out of a minicab shop in London for just hinting I was going somewhere else. Don't let the occasionally bad mannered seller stop you from asking. Most reputable sellers will only be too happy to tell you about their competitors and what makes them different and better.

There is no harm asking someone about their competition. In fact, you might find out some really valuable information. Just remember to check out their information to insure that it is just not the result of bad blood within their market. Regardless, of what they say it might just teach you something you did not know about their business. The person might also use this as an opportunity to take you back to choice number 1 again and open up an opportunity for negotiation.

They need to sell a product to remain in business

The same rules apply when you have a tangible product, like a camera. You can enter the same basic dialog as you find in the sale of a service. The main difference here is that the seller may have fewer methods of altering the features or the offering of the basic product.

One way dealers in the camera business, differentiate their offer from their competitors is to package accessories. In addition, they might add or subtract warranties to impact the price they can offer, or emphasize their service and support abilities.

They need to get what you have

This is often the most neglected point in any negotiation, and this is a point you should never forget. Whenever we think of buying anything, we immediately focus on what we want. Our goal is to get the sofa, the camera, the job, etc. We try to visualize the item we want. We make mental notes on the amount we want to pay for it. We are so concerned about our desire and our needs that we forget the other party has needs as well.

This oversight not only ignores the other party; it also reduces the flexibility and control that you have in achieving your goal. You must learn to win twice—once for you and once for the other side. This is an important concept we will cover later in the book. Your goal is to make sure that both parties are happy with the result of the negotiation. If you fail to consider the real needs of the other party, you stand a good chance to lose in your effort to get what you want.

Learning about the other party's needs should be on the top of your list of things you should research in preparing for a negotiation.

In a situation where you are buying something and all you are offering is money, you may think that your homework is done, but it isn't. Take a moment to examine WHY the seller needs your money.

For example, if his store is bulging with customers, do they really need your purchase that bad?

This may seem a ridiculous question, but it will impact your ability to negotiate. If I have fifty customers begging me for my product or service, I do not have to take the time to deal with you. Why waste a minute of my time? This is not a good situation for someone who is looking to buy.

On the other hand, many businesses finance their inventory. If the product you want has been sitting on the shelf for a long time, it might be costing the seller to keep it there. If the item you want to buy hasn't moved out of their stock, they might be willing to part with it for less money.

What about overall economic demand for what you want? If the general economy has been down, the vendor might be afraid to hold too much in stock. As I write this, the demand for personal computers (PCs) is down quite a lot. Vendors are offering discounts that would have seemed crazy just a year ago. Their need is to get rid of the stock they have quickly. Each sale to one of their competitors represents a loss of income to them. You might want a new PC, but they NEED your money to stay in business.

This is what I mean about focusing on what they need. In this environment, they need your money to keep their doors open. Your money represents not only its cash value, but also the blood that is needed to keep their business alive. This gives you a significant advantage when you are interested in buying what this person is selling.

Remember the shelf space argument. Maybe the item you are interesting in buying is taking valuable shelf or selling space away from them that they could utilize more effectively to move other products. Many large consumer durable sellers offer extended terms, like "buy it now and pay 6 months later," to just keep the stock moving out and off the selling floor. If the object of the seller is to move out the product, you might be able to negotiate better terms for yourself as long as you help them move it.

Negotiation is a customary way of doing business

It never ceases to amaze me that people will often ignore the obvious. There are just some products and services where negotiation is expected, whether you know it or not.

Even though car dealers consistently refers to their "deals" in radio, newspaper, and television advertising, many people want to just get the price, pay it and be done with it. The fact of the matter is that "dealing" is a way of life in the car business. The reason car dealers are the best negotiators is that the art of negotiation is their customary way of doing business. They are the best educated in the art of negotiation—either through education, books, or everyday experience.

A fundamental part of your research should determine the rules of engagement regarding the purchase you want to make. You need to know if negotiating is a customary way of doing business for the good or service that you want to buy. If people are used to negotiation as part of the rules of engagement, you should be ready to negotiate. If the customary way of doing business is to avoid negotiation at all cost, you will have a much harder time trying to negotiate. Notice, I said it would be a harder job. You might just be successful at a negotiation where it is unexpected, but the likelihood is less.

Houses, cars, and major consumer durables are usually sold by people who are ready, and usually very able, to negotiate. You should not deprive them of this opportunity. In fact, just about every move you make will be thought to be part of your negotiation strategy.

I found this out accidentally a number of years back. There used to be a true cut-rate dealer of consumer electronics in Newark, New Jersey that would offer the lowest prices for miles around. I walked in once with a friend who was interested in buying some stereo equipment. This young salesman, who we ended up referring to as "Crazy Mitch," started to follow me around. I stopped to look at a pair of speakers, and Mitch ran up to me brandishing his pocket calculator.

"I can let you have them for…" Mitch said—frantically banging out the digits 149.00 on his calculator and shoving it into my face.

"Thanks, but no," I said seemingly indifferent. In fact, I was indifferent since I had no intention of buying anything that day—remember I was helping a friend.

Five minutes later, Mitch appeared again.

"Look, I want you to buy those speakers, how's this…" this time shoving that calculator into my face with 129.00 displayed.

"Thanks again, but I'm not—"

This time Mitch didn't even wait the five minutes.

"Okay, Okay…" This time the calculator showed 99.00.

This time I finally convinced him to leave me alone. There is a lesson for you, though, in that experience. Here was an environment where people were expected to be open to negotiation. Mitch was misinterpreting all of my signals to mean that I was waiting for his best price. He thought I was just being tough on the negotiation!

If I had been in the market for those speakers, I might have been happy to pay 149.00 for them, but wouldn't it have been better if I got them at his rock-bottom price of 99.00? I'll bet that Mitch sells a lot of profitable speakers at 149.00 to those who come in with a non-negotiable attitude. I wonder how many people wait for that third and last price. After that experience, I would have gone for his fourth or fifth price.

The lesson is simple and has been repeated throughout the ages in the aphorism "in Rome, do as the Romans." If they expect you to negotiate, don't disappoint them.

Sellers would be wise to recognize this as well. I was once involved selling expensive telecommunications gear. Freshman sales reps would often want to offer their customers their most discounted price to secure the deal quickly. This would often fail to work for the following reason.

Let's say that vendor A comes in and says the price is $100,000 and that is their best price. After some minor haggling, the customer gets the price down to $85,000. Then vendor B appears with a price of $100,000. Once again, vendor B declares what a bargain it is for $100,000. Once again, the customer succeeds in negotiating the price down—getting it down to $75,000 this time.

Now vendor C, the freshman sales rep, comes to the table. Thinking that the customer doesn't want to haggle, the rep declares that with all of the discounting allowed they have come to a price of $85,000.

In fact, the other two vendors have trained this customer that the first offer is not the lowest. When the customer starts to negotiate, the rep has nowhere to go. The customer is disappointed and the rep is flabbergasted that the customer doesn't see that this first offer is the lowest price. This ends up a no win/no win negotiation.

If the seller or the buyer is used to negotiating, do not disappoint them. You might think that you can cut right to the best price, but in their world and from their experience in it, how can you expect them to know that this time is different?

My vote is to err on the side that says these people want to negotiate. You can almost always laugh off and apologize for an inappropriate attempt. If they are expecting to negotiate all along, you should be ready to start the ball rolling.

4

Start at the Right Price

Sellers manipulate you with the "limited edition" concept

Every now and then, the news reports a story of some buyer paying millions of dollars at an auction for a Van Gogh painting. Unless you are an art connoisseur, you probably wonder why someone would pay such extravagant amounts for an aged piece of canvas on a wooden frame.

It might be a beautiful picture, but if you think about it, some art lover has probably already made a fine reproduction that is just as beautiful. If the buyer just wanted that beautiful picture, he could have saved a few million by buying the reproduction.

There is but one unmistakable reason for owning the original Van Gogh. If you, the buyer, want the actual canvas with the very paints that Van Gogh touched with his own hand—perhaps mixed with his own sweat—you need to get this painting. In fact, since Van Gogh laid down his brushes long ago, and many of his works adorn museum walls, this might be your only opportunity to secure a Van Gogh work. This is your chance, possible your only chance in a lifetime, to get this specific example of his work.

Unfortunately, you are not the only one who wants it. That museum, which recently received a huge endowment, has a representative at that auction. With a cavalier attitude their representative is ready to act like he is spending his own money to get that painting at all costs. Add a couple of hundred other potential and eager buyers

from all around the world and you soon have the makings of a digni-
fied sale, that is the art world's equivalent of a starving mob who will
go all out to get for themselves a last, remaining crust of bread.

It's that "last crust of bread" mentality that is behind the concept of
the limited edition. Sellers use this concept to transform your desire in
their product from a vague interest into a burning need. It is the basic
law of supply and demand sharpened to the point of your purchase. If
food is in limited supply and you are starving, hunger has increased its
demand, you will pay whatever price you have to get it.

Fortunately, the reverse of that law is also true. If you are filled to
the brim with all you can eat, the price for that additional dessert
becomes unimportant. It no longer has immediate value for you. A
reproduction Van Gogh costs much less because, by its very definition,
it can be reproduced again and again, until everyone that wants one has
one.

You need to fully understand the importance of this concept before
you think of buying anything. For it is you, the buyer, who determines
what something is really worth and it is you who sets the price. Let's
repeat that for emphasis.

You set the price!

Most people think that it is the seller that determines the price. After
all, every car has a sticker on a window that has the manufacturer's suggested retail price. The person selling a house gives you the price he
wants for it. Even every can of beans in the supermarket has a price
sticker that was put there by someone other than you.

But this is all an illusion. Whether it is a car, a house, a piece of furniture or a glass of lemonade from a five-year-old street vendor, you
determine what something is worth and the price that you will pay for
it.

If you leave that can of beans on the shelf too long, that price will
drop. Ok, you might not want to eat them when the price drops to
zero, but consider the car market. Notice that a 2002 car model price

changes when the 2003's hit the showroom. Even before that happens, if the dealer can sell you that car for $2000 off of the sticker price, what is the price of the car? Simple math:

Sticker price - the $2000 = the new price.

Now many buyers will puff themselves up and say that they bought a car that was worth X, but paid $2000 less. But was the car really worth X? If it was, why didn't you pay X?

The reason is clear. Go back a few paragraphs. You decide what something is worth. You set the price.

Remember, in the introduction, when my mother wanted the tree removed. The first service wanted $4,500. She ended up paying $1,500. What was the job really worth? $1,500. You see the buyer sets the price and the value of the purchase.

Why do sellers seem to set prices? Their actions make you believe that they have the power to do this. All they really do is write the price THEY WANT down on some piece of paper or a sign. Why do they do this? It should be obvious now that this tactic of setting a price is usually a very successful one.

How many times have you taken that can of beans to the checkout and asked them to lower the price? It doesn't happen often. People usually function automatically. They see the number and pay it. Sellers just love it. Sellers TRY to set the price because unthinking buyers usually just pay what they ask. You would be surprised how many cars go for the sticker price.

Diamonds are a good case in point. The diamond market is tightly controlled by the sellers. These sellers limit the amount of diamonds sold to make sure that the overall market prices stay above a certain level. True they are scarce, but the supply is limited further by industry practices.

I used to sell diamonds and people would often ask what a particular stone is worth. I would always say that it is worth what you want to pay for it. If someone said, but isn't it really worth a lot more? I would say yes, if you could induce someone else to buy it for more. What I was really saying is that the value only truly goes up if they find another buyer who will pay more, because **the buyer sets the price**.

Back to the Van Gogh, there have been many times in the art market when an auction purchaser has seen the price of his investment drop when he tries to resell it. This happens when the new buyer sets a lower price. Maybe it just wasn't worth the same amount to the new buyer. The market will often use this new purchase to reevaluate the stated value of similar objects. Again, the market is recognizing the new price set by the newest buyer. I'm sure you get the idea by now.

This knowledge should be used to empower you as the buyer. After this point, you should never again assume that the price or value of something is set by someone else. It is up to you. This is secret knowledge, however, and should never be disclosed to a seller in any transaction. Remember he has his "tricks-of-the-trade," this is one of yours.

Your objective as the buyer is to set the price of whatever you want to buy to the lowest amount you can. Let's consider some examples where sellers will use this concept of limited editions to further manipulate you into paying the prices that they set.

The most notable example of the limited edition technique is obviously with a limited edition. Almost all product sellers produce a product that they call the limited version of their typical product. Sometimes they will label them with additional indications of limited availability. One favorite indicator is listing an edition number.

For example, a watchmaker who puts a mark of, lets say, "1/5000" on the back of a watch case—is effectively saying that this is number one in an edition of 5000. This engraving is offered to the public as proof of its limited availability. If you are a collector of such watches, it is up to you, as the buyer, to determine the true validity of the limited edition status of the watch.

For example, if there are 25,000 avid collectors of this manufacturer's watches, it might be worth paying more for one of an edition of 5000. This population count might indicate that there will be a great deal of demand for one of these. But what if there are only 4000 that would really be interested in this model. Five thousand watches chasing 4000 buyers may mean that this limited edition is going to be left with 1000 leftover watches lying around.

You might have noticed a similar phenomenon around Christmas time when various Christmas tree ornament manufacturers announce the limited availability of specific ornaments. That ornament that is priced, due to its "limited edition" status, for $50 before Christmas, can often be found on the leftover tables for $12 the day after Christmas.

So how do you separate the bargain from the future loss? Research. Learn enough about the market that the edition is released into BEFORE buying it on the strength of that limited edition label. Then, as always, offer what YOU think it is worth.

There is another type of "limited edition" that everyone will run into at least once when purchase anything. This is the attempt by a seller to create a limited edition in the mind of the purchaser on the spot.

For example, I have not yet left a car dealer without hearing at least one of the following phrases:

1. I have three other people interested in this particular car.

2. This is the last one we have like this.

3. I can't hold this too long, it is very popular.

4. Better hurry, I can't hold this price after today.

It might not have a label that says "limited edition," but they are presenting it to you just the same. Every one of these phrases is designed to turn the car you looked at into a limited edition in your mind. Each is targeted to turn your interest into a true desire and finally into a desperate need. Don't let it happen to you

If a seller has turned your interest into a truly "must have" desire, you have lost the deal right then and there. Let's go back to the crust of bread example. Are you really going to hold out for an extra penny for that last crust of bread if you are starving—if you really, really need it? Hardly. You can bet the dealer knows this, and is using your desire to make the sale right there and then.

This is the way many sellers set the price and win. If the seller sees you got to have this one, he also sees fat commissions in his pocket.

The key to defeating the limited edition technique is to show the seller that you have not moved to the "need" stage. You need to make him believe that you do not really need the item that bad. Even if you are at the point where you are desperate, you have to maintain an outward appearance that shows you can get by without it.

When the dealer explains to you that this is the last one, thank him, say you appreciate knowing that, but you don't really need it now. You can wait for the next one.

Many items that are in short supply with one dealer are available from another. I was recently helping a relative who wanted a green Honda Civic. A dealer explained to me that he had only one green one left. That's OK, I said, the color is not that important. The price was the most important item for me. I knew that if we got the price settled (my real need), he might give me the green one, and if not, I would find a dealer who had the green one for the price I was ready to pay.

You see, many limited supply items are only limited by the particular seller you visit. Others might have the item you want by the truckload, and are looking for a way to unload them cheaply.

Your best advantage in any purchase is the knowledge garnered by good research. You can learn if the item you want is truly limited by just conducting a little research. Go to the library, look in books, magazines, newspapers, or just search through the Internet. A few minutes spent on understanding the price range of the items you want to buy can save you money. If the item is sold by many dealers, than even items in limited supply become negotiable to the person who is willing to try to see which dealer will offer the lowest price or the best terms.

Of course, you will come across a time when it will be very difficult to negotiate for a low price if the item you want is sold by only one source or if it is truly limited. Even if you have to deal with single source, the game is not quite over. There are times when the supply is limited, but the demand is limited as well.

Remember the limited edition Christmas ornament example mentioned above. Sometimes the manufacturers advertise that they only have created 15,000 of the particular item and sell them at a premium price—at least before Christmas. How can they be sold so easily the week after Christmas for 50% off?

Clearly, they overestimated the demand and are left with stock they cannot sell without discounting the price. Your research should indicate not only the limit of the supply, but also the limit of the demand. If you know the demand is weak, you can usually use that knowledge to drive to a lower price. In fact, you can ask the person selling it if they really had any recent offers for the item. They may say yes, but, if they haven't, your question might just get them thinking that this is really their best chance to sell it—now.

Timing is very much the key to saving money on limited editions. Changing conditions can often impact your ability to drive to a lower price. With the proliferation of digital photography, it will be interesting to see if the market will be flooded with film based cameras—even those that were formerly in limited supply. Anecdotal evidence in late 2002 indicate that the prices of used film camera have begun to drop based upon the influx of all of the cameras placed on the market by those upgrading to digital.

Past history of the collectables business indicates cycles of change in both rarity and scarcity. High prices often bring out items thought lost to history. When all of the major collectors have secured their example, prices tend to fall off as the demand decreases. After a time, new collectors often bring up demand and prices climb again. Part of your research should be targeted to see what part of the cycle you are in when buying what you consider a limited edition.

That is really the last word on this topic. If you are truly interested in buying a limited edition of anything, make sure YOU know it is limited. Don't let sellers use this concept to manipulate your purchase. You must judge how far you want to go in securing the item. Your knowledge, not the salesperson's, should be your guide.

Once you set the price you want to pay, you should also determine if there are any other criteria that will impact your purchase.

5

Look Beyond Price to Be a Better Negotiator

Obviously, you want to pay the right price, but focusing too heavily on price can lead you to overlook other issues or benefits. There are a large number of factors that revolve around the item you want to buy. You need to examine all of the factors surrounding your purchase to truly get the best deal.

In fact, you should be glad that price is not the only factor when you are looking to negotiate for the purchase of a good or service. You improve your chances of negotiating the deal you ultimately want, when you can identify additional factors to use within the negotiation. Before entering any negotiation, you should take some time to identify and make a list of any of the factors that exist, outside of price, that are part of the overall purchase.

For example, in purchasing a camera you can obviously start the list with two items:

1. Camera

2. Price

If you take a moment to think about it in detail though, there are other considerations which should make the list. Here are some examples:

3. New or used. Obviously, you will pay less if you are the second buyer. In some cases, you can purchase a demonstrator model

(demo). If you are willing to accept a used or demo piece of equipment, you may be able to use this flexibility to save even more money in the negotiation

4. Accessories. Does this seller sell all of the original equipment with the camera? Some dealers will sell you the original manufacturer's body, but will package another manufacturers lens with the camera. This might allow them to offer you a lesser price, but it might also offer you an inferior product. I usually buy a camera based upon the lens that it comes with. Personally speaking, I would not want to save money by not getting the camera and lens combination that I want. Additionally, there may be other accessories—filters, film, cable release, case, etc. that this vendor provides as part of the price. These also usually increase his return on the sale. Many times they will increase your cost over the price you wanted to pay. It is up to you to determine what accessories the dealer is bundling with the product you want to buy. It might be a good deal, or you might save more by buying these accessories later. In addition, you might be able to save money by having the dealer back out the accessories. But be careful with this strategy, smart dealers will use their ability to trade off these accessories to maintain the price they want to get. Don't let this seller strategy reduce the final package you want for the price you want to pay. Negotiate the overall price first as far as you can, before offering to give back accessories for further price reductions.

5. Warrantee or Guarantee. Is the seller offering the original manufacturers warranty or his own? Is the product a gray market product where the warrantee requires you to ship your camera to some faraway, foreign location for service? How long is the warrantee? The answers to these questions will impact not only the price, but your cost of ownership. It is a good idea to understand up front what your warrantee coverage brings you.

6. Extended Warrantees. Generally, these are money makers for the seller. Thankfully, in this age of sophisticated, quality manufacturing, most products that are doomed to fail will do so during the original warrantee period. That is why this often becomes a money maker for the seller. They end up selling insurance that rarely will produce a claim. Although, you need to beware of new technologies that are costly to repair or replace. Sometimes you will need to bite the bullet and buy that extended warrantee. One of the most successful tactics of selling insurance is that the sellers can point to instances where it has been clearly worth it. You should do a little leg work on your own (don't wait for the seller to give you his reasons) to understand the risks of buying or not buying the extended warrantee. If the risk of needing it is high and the costs of being without it are high, buy it. Just make sure that you are making an informed decision on your own

7. Service. Whether you buy the insurance or not, you will want to know who will do the service. This might be important to you. You might want the convenience of being able to take it right back to the seller. Then again, you might not care. I have bought cameras from vendors who were thousands of miles away from me because this was not an important issue for me. You might not feel the same. The service details should still be included on your list, even if it is not important to you. You might be able to use it as a point to abandon to the seller for a lower price.

8. Convenience. In our age of overnight delivery services, I am willing to look anywhere in the country to save some money. These companies have made the distant store seem like it is right in the neighborhood. Sometimes I am willing to pay additional shipping costs if I save on the price of the product itself. Some people feel more comfortable if they can look right into the eyes of the seller. They only want to shop somewhere where they can be there in person. Often, this person-to-person convenience costs more. For example, there is a camera shop right in my neighborhood that

I can buy from, but on balance, his prices are usually a little higher than what I can get from a major city camera dealer. His business is built on convenience. If I need some film within the next few minutes, I know I can walk down to his shop and get it. I don't mind paying a dollar more since no one can beat the convenience of just running into his shop. You need to consider the convenience of dealing with your seller as another criterion in your negotiation.

9. Time. Like convenience, time has its own benefits and detractions. Overnight delivery can save time, but it can cost extra. Is it worth waiting a few more days or will the seller absorb the cost of the overnight service? Time of delivery is one consideration, but what about the time required to negotiate. I helped my father-in-law shop for a car. I helped him save over $5000, but it took five months to get the car. He tells people that he saved $1000 for each month he waited. He had the time to wait. What if you don't? You should determine how much time and negotiation you are willing to take to get the price you want. Even if this is not on your list, you had better believe it is on the list of the seller. Sellers often use your "I want it now" enthusiasm to close the sale. Try to keep your eagerness to yourself. In most cases the lower price goes to the most patient. Understand your time constraints before you begin any negotiation.

There are probably other points that are important to both the buyer and seller. In this instance, we have pinpointed nine different issues that can impact the success or failure of this negotiation for a camera. You might find fifteen issues to consider about the item you want to buy. This is an exercise that pays off. You gain power and confidence by brainstorming and researching any factors that you can identify before entering into a negotiation.

The reason you need to take the time to compile such a list should be obvious by now. Many people make the mistake of focusing solely on price and product in determining the success or failure of a negotiation.

For the seller, a strict focus on price and product reduces the opportunities for any other compromise. The buyer also paints himself into a corner with the same plan. After all, if the seller won't compromise on price, where else can you go? By building your list of factors beyond price, you have multiple issues and opportunities to negotiate over before getting to the price issue.

If you hit a wall on the price issue, you can either stand there and beat your head against it or find a way around the wall. These items give you the chance to go around the wall. As vendors invest their time with you over the other factors, usually they will come around on improving the overall deal so you say yes and get more for your money.

Let's take "time" as one example from our list. It might be emotionally difficult for you to wait for the dealer to cut his price, but while you are waiting you still have your money (or you don't have a credit card payment). Time for you, the buyer, is frequently only an inconvenience.

In the meantime, the seller has an item in inventory. It might be taking up valuable shelf space where he can place something that will move faster. In all likelihood, he has probable financed his inventory. That means that each day it sits on his shelf, it is costing him interest payments. Not to mention, if he is in business to sell, each day it sits on his shelf is a day he is not making money on it.

Often these conditions will force the seller to make the offer I am sure you have heard in the past. "If you buy it right now, I'm prepared to offer you a discount." Even if the seller does not make that offer you can help point it out.

I once saw an expensive high-end VCR in an electronics store that was marked for clearance. Rather than pay the clearly very reasonable price that was on it. I got into a discussion with the seller about how long it had been on the shelf. I said I was interested, but that the price was still a little too expensive. He signaled that he was willing to negotiate by immediately dropping his price for me. He countered that it was very reasonable considering what it originally cost.

I agreed with him, it was now an even better deal, but I wanted to see if I could save just a little more. I mentioned that I was concerned that it looked like it had been out on the shelf for a while. I said that it must be taking up space that he could use to display a newer model. He mentioned that that was true, but he still felt his price was reasonable.

I then said that I was really interested in this machine and said that if he could meet me at my price, which was about $50 less than his posted number, I would take it right now and he could free up that shelf space for something else. He thought for a moment and then made a counter offer that was about $25 less than his posted price. I accepted. He was happy to get rid of it for the $25 difference, and I was happy to buy it at a price that would have been unobtainable anywhere else.

By focusing on a time factor, price became more flexible and less of a block to the deal. I also focused on the fact that it was not exactly the same as a brand new, in the box purchase. This should also impact the price. In addition, I agreed with the seller about his conditions along the way, but stated my objections as we went along.

This is also a very good strategy to employ when negotiating. When people hear the word "NO," they usually stop listening. You could actually say no, and then agree with what they are saying, and find instances where they never hear any of the further agreement. The word "NO" just sets up a barrier in their mind.

You need to learn how to say "No" and yet keep the negotiation open. You can do this easily by finding something in what they have said that you agree with, but expressing reservation about the part you disagree about.

Let's compare two sentences to see what I mean.

"No, your price is too high"

"Yes, I agree that you are making a good offer, but I still think that there is some room to negotiate."

In the first sentence, the seller might not hear anything after the word "no." No means that there is no place to go. In the second sentence, I am still saying no, but I am also giving the seller another chance to come up with something that can keep the negotiation open.

Seek something to say that expresses agreement with the seller. Obviously he is taking sometime to work with you; give him some benefit for his work. You might not be able to agree with anything he said, but don't let that stop you. Find something to agree upon.

For example, "I agree that the camera is really nice, but I need to find some way to save some money on the purchase.

Here you are agreeing with the object versus what the seller has said. I still avoided the use of the word no and any point of heated disagreement.

Sometimes, you might feel that the seller is rude to you or angers you. This is still no excuse to try to pay him back with your words. You have a couple of choices, you can be polite and disengage (remember, you may want to reengage sometime in the future when his rudeness has dissipated) or you can still be polite and pursue the negotiation in spite of his rudeness. If you chose the latter, it is still preferable to stay above his level and keep your cool.

Most people forget to think when they are being insulted. If you don't keep thinking about the situation versus the insult, you will miss the opportunities that might surface from the difficulty.

I once attended a meeting of a service organization. This group had recently lost a number of regular maintenance customers to lower priced service providers that did not have the means to fully service their customer's problems under their contracts. That is why the service organization's competition was able to offer a lower price.

It soon became evident that some of these lost customers would need service from our organization because the competing service provider had some holes in their coverage. Some of our organization's people suggested that they put the problems of these returning customers at the back of the list of those they would get to first. They wanted to pay back those customers that had deserted their maintenance offerings.

"Why should I treat them as good as my regular maintenance paying customers?" was the cry. The meeting was degrading into a high school football rally.

I couldn't take it. I stood up and stopped the meeting. I pointed out that their emotional payback was only going to hurt their business further. Yes, the customer would pay by the delay, but the customer would also see our tardiness as another reason to avoid our organization.

By attending to the lost customers' problems quickly, they had this opportunity to show that our maintenance pricing included fast and effective response to ALL of their problems. By rushing to their aid, they paid back the customer with kindness, and they now had the opportunity to have that kindness repaid by the customer returning. As an added bonus, the non-maintenance contract work that we did for the customer was already billable. So we were paid for the work and we had the opportunity to win back the customer. In the meantime, the customer won by getting the problem fixed.

This is another example where price is not the only object. Service is also important. In short, everything on your list is important. It should be obvious by now that you need to take the single object of your negotiation and turn it into a package of goods. You can use your list to compile all of the items within that package and then set a price that you will pay for that package. If all you want to pay is the lowest price, then be prepared to trade away items from that package to get the price you want.

Trade off the items you have little interest in for the ones that you really need. Negotiation is a game of give and take. By going beyond price, you give yourself more chances to give and more benefits to gain. In addition, the old rule that "it is better to give than receive' gains an added boost through your knowledge of those items that you can give away easily.

By giving up something in the process, you also help the seller win in the negotiation. This is an important concept that buyers also fail to learn. When the seller wins, you win. You help to establish grounds for future business, even if it does not seem likely at the present time. You only truly win, when you win twice.

6

Prepare to Win—Twice!

You win! How does that feel?

Even it you are one of those people who claim that winning has passed you by, try to think about it. I am sure if you search your life long enough, you can find something you won. It might have been a dollar win from a scratch-off lottery ticket. Whatever you won, just try to remember the feeling you had.

It was great. Was it not? Even if you won something small or insignificant, the feeling of winning something is unmistakable. You want to tell your spouse, your mother, even your dog. It seems like the air is fresher, and your life takes on new meaning.

How about the other side of the coin? Do you remember the feeling of losing? It's not quite the same. You might laugh off a bulk mail sweepstakes telling you that you are a millionaire, but that lottery ticket which missed a fortune by a number or two might have caused you some distress. When professional sports teams fritter away a game in the final seconds, they leave hundreds of fans feeling upset and hurt. Let's face it. There is no fun in losing.

Don't worry though. The skills that you learn here are designed to make you a winner at every negotiation you enter and every purchase you have to make. Even if you have never won before, this is going to be your moment. Prepare to win, but prepare to win twice.

Every time you win at a negotiation, you need to win twice—once for you and once for the other person. What other person are we talking about? It should be obvious that the other person is the one on the other side of the negotiation. You need to be just as concerned about the other person as you are about yourself.

This may seem counterintuitive to you. After all, in most games between two people, one is usually the winner and one is the loser. If you focus on negotiating to win at all costs, you may be so consumed with your result that you overlook what happens to the other guy. This is a serious mistake.

You know how it feels to lose. This is what the other person is going through right now. Why would you want to do that to another person? You must have lost at something in life, don't think that you need to do this to someone else so you can win.

If you make that furniture dealer feel that he never wants to deal with the public again after dealing with you, how do you think he will respond when you come back when you find that minor defect? If you are lucky, he might ignore you. If your luck is not quite good, he might offer to help you now by seeking every single opportunity for retribution.

Like a fighter that is intent on revenge against a previously winning opponent, you set yourself up for future trouble if you insist on demanding that every win you have is at a substantial cost or loss to your opponent.

As a matter of fact, think about that word "opponent." Is that really what the other person is in a negotiation? According to the dictionary, an opponent is "one who opposes another or others in a battle, contest, controversy, or debate." I don't know about you, but frankly I do not want any seller to oppose me. In fact, I do not want any negotiation to be a battle, a contest, a controversy, or a debate.

I like to think of sellers as very nice people, who are trying to make me happy with their product or service and gain something from the transaction for themselves. I will just be happier if I can get it for less or make a better deal. My goal is to make them happy to sell to me. Negotiation is a game where both people can win. Many writers in the field stress this as win/win negotiating. You should always take advantage of this ability to make the other person a winner also. You should always prepare to win twice.

You see the other side has positive needs as well. The sale should make them happy, too. It brings them your cash to pay for their groceries, their next vacation, and their kid's education. Maybe you solved their overstock problem, or reduced their business debt. Whatever it is, try to identify something that your opposite will gain from the negotiation and help him to do it as best as you can.

If you focus on the seller's needs, as much as your own, and help them achieve their needs, they will win and so will you. If you focus on treating the other side fairly, you have a good shot that they will treat you fairly as well. In fact, the seller is just that, the nice person on "the other side." Make the result of your deal, a happy result for the other side as well.

The alternative will not go unpunished. If you leave a trail of losers and destruction behind you, you better believe it will finally catch up to you—and perhaps when you cannot afford it.

NEVER, NEVER, NEVER adopt a win/lose mentality.

The art of negotiation is in the skill of the compromise. Successful compromise means that both parties may not get <u>everything</u> that they originally wanted but that both achieved a practical number of their needs.

For example, you may not want to pay top dollar for that product or service, and the dealer should not always expect to receive the top dollar to stay in business. On the other hand, you need to keep the dealer in business. More dealers mean more competition, and free competition often leads to better prices for many.

Most dealers will be happy to receive a <u>reasonable</u> profit on the items they sell. Occasionally, they may be willing to take a loss to achieve some other aim. These aims may include clearing out old stock, gaining new shelf space for other items, or just making needed cash for the day. If you find the dealer very willing to negotiate, he probably has one of these aims in sight as his need. If you find that he doesn't take kindly to the negotiation process, move on.

There is always someone who will be willing to bargain. Don't try to force someone to negotiate if they do not want to. You will become frustrated and they will become angry. It is not worth it.

If the other party is willing to negotiate, pay careful attention to signals indicating that they are getting angry or getting very worried. If the other party is genuinely disturbed by the negotiation, stop. Ask the other party if they are ok. Ask why they are upset. Probe, but gently. If the other party is truly upset, back off. You do not want to win at a negotiation and make the other party suffer. If the other party is under distress, be prepared to walk away.

It is good to ask questions to gather more information and to check on your progress in making the deal. It is also a good way to verify the signals that you are getting. Beginning negotiators have to be careful to differentiate a real signal of distress from a feigned signal. After all, if I can make you think that I cannot go as low as you want, you might stop the process and buy it at the price I am at.

If the answer to your question indicates that the struggle is still over the product, it may be a feigned signal. Ask what the other person thinks is fair compromise. This might prompt them to get back into the negotiation with a counter offer.

On the other hand, if the person pushes back and refuses to make any counteroffer, this might be their way of saying they do not want to proceed. Do not make them feel bad, just offer to back off. Being polite in a negotiation is good business.

The other person might just ask for time; give it to them. They might have to find how your offer can satisfy their needs. The best part of backing off politely is that you now have an opportunity to go back in the future to reopen the negotiation.

I recently backed off politely on the purchase of a camera lens, only to find the seller consummated a sale with someone else. I was disappointed, but soon after learned that the buyer, who beat me to the deal, backed off—rudely! I contacted the seller who now offered the same lens to me for fifty dollars less than the original price. I doubt the buyer I originally lost to will have the same chance. I especially noted the seller's comments on the rudeness of the original buyer. I am pleasant and polite as a matter of my belief and upbringing. If you find you need a good business reason to be that way, this is it.

7

Avoid Major Sales Traps

Watch out for sellers who exploit your fear of walking away

The limited edition strategy ultimately targets a fear that both you and the seller have—the fear of walking away with no one buying anything. If a seller convinces you that this is the one you need, you may have reached the point where your legs become powerless. It could still be too expensive for you, but a good seller will find a way for you to buy it.

You can charge the purchase. Instead of paying a thousand dollars cash, you put it on your credit card and pay $20 a month. You can afford $20 a month. Can't you? Forget that, with interest, you will end up paying three times the thousand by the time you pay it off. The fact is a good seller will find someway to get it off his hands and into yours.

Whatever the argument he makes, you are probably making a few of your own. Whether you are justifying in your mind the cash required or are thinking of how you can extend the payments, you should really be on the seller's payroll at this point because you just went to work for him. You are on his side looking for every possible way for him to make the sale—why shouldn't he pay you for that!

He has successfully manipulated you with your fear of walking away. Regardless how you look at it, he has convinced you that IF YOU WALK, YOU LOSE. He might even tell you that if he notices your foot so much as twitch. In fact, at this point, he has probably made you fear that HE might walk away. If you are sincerely interested in buying the object of your negotiation, and this is the only seller, you might be thinking just that.

Your fear of loss is heightened. You lose if you walk. You lose if he changes his mind, and refuses to sell it to you. At this point someone should knock you upside the head to shift your focus off yourself, your needs, and your fears. Recover your senses and take a look at the first sentence in this chapter. Remember that the first sentence said that BOTH you AND THE SELLER have this fear.

Buyers often overlook the fact that the seller ALSO loses when the buyer walks away. If you become anxious that you might be losing something by walking, you would do well to not only recognize this fact, but to keep it firmly fixed in your mind. Let's repeat that for emphasis:

THE SELLER LOSES WHEN YOU WALK AWAY.

Consider that sentence carefully. You might be fearful that the seller will walk, but recognize that by just engaging in a sales dialog with you he is interested in selling his product or service. No matter how rare his product or service is, if he is talking to you about selling it, he has a strong, vested interest in finding a buyer. If he has invested even a few minutes in talking to you about it, he must either be looking for a new friend or really considering you as a potential buyer. If it is the latter, he will lose if you walk. This gives you power, and power is what you want to control in any negotiation.

The more the seller invests in conversing with you, the more he is investing in the concept that you will be the buyer. I have seen this work to my advantage many times.

For example, there are times when I have returned to a particular store a few times to clearly show my interest in a product. I make sure I hunt out the same salesperson so he gets to know me and know that I am very interested. Each time I meet him, that salesperson now is investing some more time with me. That investment in his time often pays off when that seller makes an offer that is lower than the offer I originally received.

This is a key point for those people who are still shy when it comes time to negotiate. If you find that you still cannot try any of the techniques in this book, because you are too shy or you feel the other techniques are too aggressive, just try this one technique.

Find something you want to buy, visit the seller, but just do not buy it yet. Single out a particular salesperson, and try making a small business relationship with him or her. Make it clear that you are interested in the product. Talk about the product. Give the salesperson a chance to explain its benefits. If the salesperson does not seem interested in the product, find another person to talk to. Sooner or later, you will find a salesperson that truly loves the product you want.

These people will practically tell you the entire evolution of the product. This is the person you want to talk to. Show that you are just as interested in it. Make conversation on the offering. Often this is enough to get a lower price. After all, don't you want others to share in the enthusiasm that you have for something. This enthusiasm has often prompted a seller to move on price as though he were finding a home for one of his children.

If the price is still too high, don't give up. Remind the seller that you are still very interested. Apologize for bothering him and thank him for his help and time. Then leave the store.

After a day or so, go back. Try to find the same person you met a few days ago. Find something new to explore about his product. Ask more questions. Let the seller talk more about it. Get them to talk. When they ask if you are going to buy it, just ask about the price again.

Sometimes they will drop it right there. Perhaps, they will offer some payment plan to enable you to afford it. Some will just say that they are sorry, but the price is the price.

Do not get discouraged. Ask if they know of a sale coming up on the item. Sometimes they will tell you right there that it will go on sale tomorrow, next week or next month.

It follows the "sorry for the child" principle. Bill Cosby had a great stand up comedy routine where he mimicked a young child asking his father for a nickel. The father is quick to say no, but then the kid persists, "but Johnny has a nickel, and Mary has a nickel, and Joey has a…" You get the idea. After a while the father feels sorry for the kid and gives it to him.

You may not get to that point of getting it for free from the seller, but after a while, a typical seller sees that that buyer is sincerely interested. At this point many a deal is struck. If you are selling something, obviously you want it to go to someone who will value it the most.

Interestingly, if the seller feels sorry for you, he also feels like he has won by doing something altruistic. The sale is no longer just a sale, but a good deed. Matching the item he is selling with someone who obviously appreciates what he is buying. If you feel bad about someone feeling sorry for you, take a step back and review the second chapter. It is quite all right to be a little embarrassed or be thought a little less of, if you get what you originally wanted at the price you want to pay. Leave the ego at the door and win.

Keep an eye out for time pressure

One of the criticisms of the earlier technique is that it takes time to frequently visit a seller. My father-in-law tells people that I saved him $5000 in buying a car, but it took five months to find the deal. He could afford the time to wait for the deal. If he couldn't wait, I am certain that he would have paid more.

Time itself is non-negotiable. Time waits for no man, but I am willing to keep an open mind. If you ever find a way to successfully negotiate against time, please let me know.

Time is a key ingredient in all negotiations. Both sellers and buyers invest time in a negotiation. Everything we do takes time, and we usually take time for granted. Time is an important value in life, much more important than money. If you have no time left in your life, all the money in the world will not buy you more. You cannot take the value of time for granted.

On a less philosophical note, though, taking time for granted often causes people to overlook the value that time has in any negotiation.

Once I was in a hotel dressing for a key business meeting. I suddenly realized that I left my neckties home. This was a meeting where business dress was essential. Fortunately, the hotel was a mile away from a shopping mall. With one hour to go before the meeting, I raced to the mall to purchase a tie. I quickly found one on a sale table that would do, bought it, put it on, and raced to the meeting.

What would have happened if the store was not having a sale?

I would have had two choices, pay what they wanted or go to the meeting tie-less (not for this customer!). Time, in the form of the time remaining before the meeting, would have made any negotiations impossible. I needed a tie and I needed it NOW.

This concept is often referred to as time pressure. Sellers exert time pressure by telling you that they will only hold the priced for a limited time. Buyers succumb to time pressure by believing them. I am sure you have seen the television commercials that scream out that you only have the next twenty minutes to call to take advantage of that offer.

I am fairly certain that if you called in 30 minutes that they will still take your money, but you better believe that they get a lot of calls in that twenty minute period from those who are afraid to lose out.

Time pressure works. That is why you consistently hear these types of time pressure offers. Time pressure destabilizes people. Watch how difficult it becomes for people to answer questions on a game show if they have only five seconds to respond. Clever, intelligent people will often forget their own address if the time pressure is severe enough. This is one selling technique that works more often than it doesn't.

There are some ways to handle time pressure as a buyer. First, just let go of the pressure entirely. Examine whether or not this is truly your only opportunity to get what you want. Could you buy it from someone else? If you could, focus on that, and take the pressure off of your self.

If you know there are other suppliers or, hopefully, many other suppliers, you can usually just use the limited time offer as a starting point for negotiations. For example, if someone says that he can offer the item to you for $200—today only, thank him, and say you still need to think about it. If he persists, remind him that the day is not over, and you will remember his offer and comeback later that day. Then check with someone else.

If the others cannot match his price, don't be afraid to go back—even if you need to go back the next day. If you do go back the next day be polite, apologize that you couldn't make it back yesterday in time, and ask him to extend you the price he offered the day before. If he says he cannot now, he is likely just being difficult. Perhaps he was never prepared to sell it to you at that price anyway.

Sometimes, sellers will give you a price that no one can offer, just to make you think that they are unlike their competitors. When you discover that no one will offer you that price, they believe that you will return anyway. At that point they can apologize that the offer expired, but make you another offer—thinking that you now believe that they are more flexible than others. I told you that these professionals are clever.

Most good salespeople will honor their earlier offer. That is why it is good to return if you find that no one can match it. You will risk meeting the one with the phony offer, but, if you do, you can easily walk away a second time.

In the meantime, let's say you do go to another vendor. You should tell the next vendor that, "The XYZ Company will sell it to me for $200," and say nothing else. After all, that was the offer, wasn't it? There is no need to tell the other company that you are under time pressure from the original supplier to make a decision today. You are not lying. You do have a valid offer from the first supplier at that price regardless of the fact that the offer expires today.

The new vendor can match the price, beat it, or call you crazy. If they call you crazy, wait before reacting to see if you are "crazy high" or "crazy low." If you are "crazy high," it's nice to know that the dealer will tell you this and be fair about it. If you are "crazy low," find out why.

Sometimes, they will explain to you why the price you are getting is impossible. Let them explain it to you. Remember, the more you know, the more information that you have, the better chance you have that you can negotiate successfully. I have actually had dealers tell me why the price I was asking was impossible to achieve, but then I beat even that price. (Importantly, I did not go back to them and rub their noses in it. Remember, be polite. You may have to meet them again some time in the future.)

With the new knowledge, you can make an educated determination of whether or not to go back to the person holding the price, or buying from the new dealer. Or you may wait.

Waiting is another way to beat time pressure. Waiting takes patience. Patience is something that most people lose when the feel they really need what they are buying. This lack of patience is what most sellers prey on.

Before you enter any serious negotiation, clearly determine how much patience you are willing to have to get what you want. Generally, if you have patience you improve your chances of getting what you want for less.

Many people would say that just is not true due to inflation, but let me show you how this can work even in inflationary times.

Let's say you want to buy a new television. The price today is $300.00. Yes, that price happens to be 20% more than the previous model. Inflation has adjusted its price upwards, but the key to my argument rests in that same sentence. What happened to the previous model?

Even in inflationary times, manufacturers bring out new models. If the 2002 model fulfills the functions that you need, you might be able to save some money by waiting until the 2003 is on the market. Most dealers must clean the shelves of the 2002's. You might have to wait some time, but time usually works in your favor if you have the patience to go with it.

Just today, I saw the price of a car, my family recently purchased, that was $800 below what we paid four months ago. I did not care because we paid a very decent price when we needed the car. If we could have waited, we would have paid less.

That purchase provides a good transition to the concept of what do you do if you cannot wait for the price to go lower. This is the art of negotiation—getting the price you want now. This is the time when you are putting the time pressure on your self.

If you are generating your own time pressure, the seller is ecstatic. That is, if he knows about it. When you are under time pressure, the key to a successful negotiation is to remember that you do not have to tell anyone about it—especially the seller. This is a secret you need to keep to yourself.

Back to the tie example, I had a single hour to get a tie and get to my meeting. Did I tell that to the store clerk? Absolutely not.

You are under no obligation to reveal to the seller the pressures you have in conjunction with the object you want to buy. Look at it this way. A car dealer does not stand there and tell you that he has to sell a car within the next two days or he misses his monthly quota. He might, if he feels you are vulnerable to sympathy, but, for the most part, sellers rarely will let you in on their time pressures. For the same reason, you do not have to let them in on your urgency. Never tell a seller that you "really need" what he is selling, even if you do really need it. Tell him you are "only interested."

The store owner, who desperately needs cash, is very unlikely to give away this high-value bargaining chip to his potential buyer. Why, then, should you, the purchaser, give out your own high-value negotiating chips. Revealing time pressure is a very valuable chip to have.

If I, the seller, know that you MUST buy my product or service quickly. I will try to stretch out the negotiation. Sooner than later, you're going to have to make a decision, and it might be at the price I want to sell it versus the price you originally wanted to pay.

This brings us to another serious reason why people lose at negotiating.

Preserve your personal information

A clever seller tries to learn all about his potential buyer in as little time as possible. Most people gladly oblige.

There really is no mystery as to why people are so free with critical information. Many people think that they can strike a better deal with the seller if they become friends with him. The reasoning is that if the person genuinely likes me, he is likely to give me the best deal. It is definitely good to remind yourself that you are trying to buy something. If you make a new friend, that's great. Just remember why you sent shopping in the first place.

Many auto dealers are the friendliest people in the world. Just look at some of the questions and typical answers they ask when you are looking at a car:

Seller: Hi, I'm Fred. You are?

Buyer: Al Jones. (Now he has your first and last name)

Seller: Looking for a new car? (Why else would you be there?)

Buyer: Yes, mine has had it. (The seller has just identified you and your time pressure; you need a new car now!)

Seller: What do you drive today? (Why are you under time pressure?)

Buyer: A 1990 Chevy. (That's it! The car is getting very old, potentially already dead)

Seller: Can I help you? (Just tell me everything else!)

Most people open up to this simple line of questioning and give the dealer everything he needs to sell you that car in the first ten minutes you meet.

You will find few experienced dealers using that last question. It is a closed question rather than an open question. A closed question elicits a "yes or no" response. An open question elicits detailed information.

To the question, "can I help you?" there is a good chance that you will answer yes or no. Yes or no does not give the experienced seller anything to work with. The strong negotiator uses open ended questions to gain information which can be used later in the negotiations.

For example, the question "What do you drive today?" cannot be answered with a yes or no. Such an answer would make no sense. You need to think for a moment and give some detail. "I drive a 1990 Chevy." This piece of information can give the experienced dealer a great point to dig deeper. "What problems have you been having with it?" Think about your answer to this one.

The answer will not only identify the time pressure you are under. (Obviously if you need a car and it is having problems, you are a prime candidate.), but it will also let the dealer know what hot buttons to press in selling you his car. A smart dealer might even know the problems that particular model is prone to and probe along those lines.

The best defense is a clear understanding of what you will not do. You will not talk too much. You will not look at this as a way to make friends. You will treat information about yourself like the money you plan to spend—give as little as you can to get what you want.

I have found that you can be polite and pleasant without having to give away a dossier about your life to a seller.

For example, when car dealers have approached me with that outstretched hand and their name, I have simply replied "hello." A couple of salespeople have persisted and asked me for my name. I have replied "I'm just looking," and they generally don't ask a second time.

You can limit answers—even to open questions. One way is to answer the question with another question. "What kind of car do you drive today?" can be met with, "I'm sorry, but does this model come with a sun roof?" Politicians do this all the time. Watch a political debate to see how you can safely answer someone's questions without actually answering their question.

Most times, a good salesperson will persist and try other open questions. Don't be intimidated. Just explain clearly and politely that you are just looking and want to consider the car you are looking at before you waste his time with your needs. At this point a good salesperson will recognize your thoughtful rejection of his advances and leave you alone. If the salesperson continues to persist, you might as well say you are not interested and leave.

If a salesperson is not mature enough to know when to back off, you should recognize that as an opportunity to back out. Some sales representatives think that intimidation is the way to sell.

Resist and avert pure intimidation

One of the most memorable off screen stories from the film *The Godfather* was the story of Johnny Fontaine's major career move. In the film, Michael Corleone tells his new girlfriend Kay that Johnny Fontaine was indentured to a big band leader who would not release him from his contract. Michael's father, Don Corleone, visited the band leader to negotiate a release for Johnny from his contract.

When money and polite conversation failed to provide a release, Don Corleone had Luca Brassi hold a gun to the head of the stubborn band leader. He explained that either his brains or his signature would go on the release contract. Needless to say, it was his signature that made it on the paper.

Unfortunately, some salespeople try similar tactics to force people to buy their product. They may not pull a gun on you, but I have heard car dealers try the following delay tactics.

When they feel they are close to a deal, they will ask you to sign an offer document and ask for a credit card to present to their manager for approval. When they return with the amazing news that their manager cannot accept such a low offer, they then continue to negotiate with you to get the some more money on the deal. When you ask for your credit card back, they say they will return it in just a minute, once they have a chance to explain their case. They think that as long as they can detain you, they might be able to get you to succumb to the higher price.

The way to avoid this type of intimidation is to just prevent it from happening. Whenever a car dealer has asked me for a check or a credit card to take in with the offer I just refuse. If he persists, I explain that I would like him to go in to the manager and just find out first if they will accept my offer.

The dealer will usually say that he cannot do this. This is their way of doing business. I just resist. I ask him what he has to lose by asking his manager with the information he already has. After a moment or two, the dealer usually follows that procedure. After all, he cannot afford to have a buyer walk away just because of some internal policy. He knows this. You should also. I have resisted this tactic every time.

I have even had one car dealer ask me for a blank check! Pleaaase!

I give him credit, though; it must have worked on someone once. Otherwise, he would have given up on that technique.

I have heard of people being held veritable hostages at time sharing and real estate deals. One time share salesman tried to keep me and my wife in his office until I heard all of his pitch. They may not pull a gun on you, but they will use every form of verbiage to keep you in your seat.

Obviously, if the object of my affection is one of a kind and I really want it, it is difficult to avoid succumbing to intimidation. The trick to avoiding this hazard is to always, always do your best to keep yourself in a position to escape. If you cannot parry the intimidation, you should just leave.

Walk away when all else fails

Walking away, under your own power, is perhaps the best way to lose at a negotiation for a product or service. Make the choice yourself to quit. After all, when you make the choice yourself to walk away, the only thing you lose is the item you wanted to buy. Let's look at what you win.

1. In the intimidation example, you win the intimidation battle. This is not an insignificant victory. By refusing to be intimidated in the negotiation, you tell the seller, that you intend remain in control of the negotiation. You have resisted an attempt to take power away from you, and you reestablish your position of power. Intimidators only gain power if they can establish control over the negotiations by keeping you intimidated.

Typically, when you say no, the intimidators increase the level of intimidation. When you get up and leave, their choice of tactics are reduced to physical restraint or begging you to stay. Obviously if you are negotiating something where physical restraint is an option, you do not want to take this option without some serious consideration. This book is designed to help you negotiate the purchase of an everyday product or service. You should study the negotiation literature further for the best thinking on how to handle life or death threats. In those instances where your safety is not in question, walking away is a clear option to stop the intimidation

2. You win by not paying more than you wanted to pay. One of the reasons many people go to auctions is to buy items below their typical retail cost. One of the reasons people leave hating auctions is that they got caught up in the bidding and "win at all costs" atmosphere in the room. They won at all costs and now regret the cost. By leaving a negotiation that is not going your way, you show that you will not succumb to that "win at all costs" mentality. You can leave confident that you did not fall prey to a higher price. As long as you are not dealing with a one of a kind item, you will often get the opportunity to try again.

If you are a bidder in on-line auctions, like EBay, a good strategy is to look over completed auctions for the items you want. You will often find that items that do not sell are often posted with

LOWER starting or "buy it now" prices subsequently. I have often gambled that the item I want will NOT sell the first time. Invariably, the owner reposts the item with a LOWER price point. Then, I will bid. Once again, sellers bank on people succumbing to time pressure or rising bids. By carefully researching the items you want, you can beat the seller's strategy almost every time.

3. You win the opportunity to someday reopen the negotiation. A lot of people think that when they leave a negotiation that the door has closed and that it will never reopen again. This is far from fact. Leaving to negotiate another day is often a very practical and positive tactic.

If you can, disengage politely. This gives you a good chance of reopening the negotiation later when you have had a chance to consider the trade offs that you would consider to win.

I remember spending time with a car dealer without positive result and then leaving politely. The following day, I called back. I mentioned that I really appreciated the time he spent with me yesterday, and that I was sorry we couldn't come to some agreement. The sales rep replied that he might be able to offer me some other incentives that were not part of yesterday's discussion. My call back told him that the investment of time that he spent with me yesterday was not yet lost. He now had another chance to win and sell me that car. My departure and return opened the door to additional incentives.

If I bought yesterday, he would have made more by ignoring those further incentives. Now that I am still a candidate, he feels he needs to pull out something new for me to get the negotiations started again. Walking away can clearly be profitable.

Now I have also experienced the dealer who, when I called back, said that that was his final offer. At his point I would still be polite and thank him again. I would also let him know that if conditions were to change and he could offer me the price I wanted, he could call me back.

You never know. You might have been at the true limit of his discount. New incentives and business conditions change all the time, however. By politely disengaging, I am still on his list of potential customers if one day he is able to meet my price.

In the each of these instances, whenever I have walked away, the experience that I have gained from the first negotiation always led to better understanding of what I needed the next time.

One day, my father-in-law went to a car dealer without me and told the dealer the price that we wanted to pay to get the car he wanted. The dealer gave my father in law his business card and wrote on it some details as to what his lowest price was. It was no where near what we wanted to pay.

The dealer told him to call me and ask me to call this dealer back. My father-in-law said that the dealer wanted to explain to me why I could not possibly buy the car we wanted for the price I was asking. This guy was sharp. He wanted to convince, not only his potential buyer that his price was right, he wanted to convince anyone who could influence his buyer.

I explained to my father-in-law that I was not going to call this dealer back. Smart as he was, I told my father-in-law that we do not want to speak to someone who would not meet our price. I wanted to spend my time talking to someone who could.

I knew at the time that my father-in-law thought I was a little bit crazy. That is; until the following month when we beat that dealer's lowest price by over $2000.00.

When we closed the deal, my father-in-law wanted me to call the dealer who said I couldn't possibly succeed. I decided not to. You should also avoid the urge to grandstand on your victory.

Remember, the <u>goal is to get the product or service for the price you are willing to pay</u>. If you need to brag, brag to your friends. Don't go out and avenge yourself against any dealer just because they tried to get a few extra dollars for themselves. Nobody likes to be told that they are wrong. You probably wouldn't like to know that the dealer took you to the cleaners, if he did. It's just not worth the effort.

In fact, the better argument is that you should always avoid making enemies. Some day that dealer might have something I want and he might then meet my price. Time and people change. Give them the opportunity to do so.

I consider Herb Cohen my mentor on negotiation skills. Herb's excellent book, *You Can Negotiate Anything*, is one of the most enjoyable books on the subject. I was once fortunate to see Herb in person at an IBM sales convention. I will never forget his presentation or his most memorable quote. He told us that in any negotiation; you have to care—**but not that much.**

This is great advice. Obviously, you need to care about getting what you want. If you care too much though, you might get angry. You might do or say something that you will regret later. Worst of all, you might pay more or get something less than what you wanted because you have clouded your mind with a "have to win" attitude. Why take that chance?

Know ahead of time how important it is to win the first time out. If it is something available from many sources, don't sweat the negotiation. Sooner or later you will find someone who will give you the price or the service you want. If at first you don't succeed—learn from that experience. Jot down on paper the price and features that the original seller offers. Take notes on his objections or restrictions. Use that information to be a better negotiator next time. The information and experience will improve your chances each time and sooner or later you will win and so will the seller.

8

Keep Your Mouth Shut!

"Shhh."

You were talking in a library, a church, a classroom or a theater. At least once in your life you heard that simple sound.

What was your reaction? Did you ignore it or did you acquiesce? Whether you were angered by the intrusion into your current actions or whether you just shut up, it probably prodded you into at least a momentary moment of silence.

That simple, "shhh," just exerted some control on your action and power grows from control.

Go into any church and just listen. Unless the choir is practicing, the overwhelming sound you hear is the silence. A single step on a marble floor echoes throughout the building. A single cough rivets your attention toward the person coughing. Not only is there power in the silence, but every sound that breaks the silence focuses your attention.

Silence brings with it both the power of its ability to focus your attention and the power of controlling your environment. The best silence begins with you. You need to learn how to keep your mouth shut whenever you negotiate. Your mouth is the greatest tool you can muster as a master negotiator, especially when you don't use it.

Good dramatists have long known the power of the silent, pregnant pause. In the movie *Casablanca*, Humphrey Bogart first sees Ingrid Bergman in Rick's Café Americain. This is the woman that has turned his life upside down. This is the woman who has focused his attention into the bottom of that whisky glass every evening since she left him. I bet there are a fair number of average Americans would have just screamed, "Hey! Where have you been?!"

Instead, he just stands there in a moment of silence that is jam packed with powerful emotion. At this point in the film, the viewer really has no idea who she is or what she did to him. Nevertheless, that silent look speaks volumes. It tells you that this is someone very important. The filmmakers have got you riveted on these two characters. You spend the whole silent interlude trying to figure out what is going to happen next.

Dramatists know that if they cease the action for a moment of silence, the action never stops. They just transferred the job of continuing the action into your head. They may know what they plan to do next—where the character is going to take you—but for a brief moment they leave it up to you to figure out. The silence draws you further and further in, as you now HAVE TO KNOW what is going to happen next.

Silence has power. Silence has control. Silence makes you work. It makes you speculate on what is real and what is not.

This is why silence is the most important and powerful technique you can bring into any negotiation. Notice, I said THE MOST IMPORTANT AND POWERFUL TECHNIQUE YOU CAN BRING INTO ANY NEGOTIATION. If you remember only one thing from this book this is it. Great negotiators learn to keep their mouth shut and develop the skill of being quiet.

Silence is frequently the most underused tool of the unsuccessful negotiator. It is also the most uncomfortable tool for a person to use. It is much easier to talk.

Try this little experiment, the next time you answer the phone, don't say a word. Just put the receiver to your ear. The person on the other side of the connection is liable to start speaking because they heard the ringing stop. After the second or third, "hello," they might hang up. If they hear some ambient noise, they may press on asking,

"Can you hear me?" If they just sit there and don't say anything, get a new friend.

Seriously, you and the other person were probably just as uncomfortable. Our life is built on conversational expectations. How many times have you answered, "Fine!" when someone casually asked how you felt today—even though you woke up sick as a dog this morning.

One of the most typical conversational expectations that have been programmed into you by our social conventions is that you say hello to the person that says hello to you. Think about your internal conversation—the one between you and yourself—when someone fails to acknowledge your greeting.

What was the matter with that person? Didn't she like me? Is she avoiding me? Is she stupid? Maybe she's mad at me? Whatever is going through your mind, until you find out for sure, you really have no idea why the other person didn't answer your hello. It could have been simple blindness.

The fact of the matter is that your ability to know the real truth is hidden by the other person's silence. Technology has not yet invented a machine that will get into another person's head and tell you what he or she is thinking. Your only recourse, when you get no answer, is to do your own speculation.

The only way to end the speculation is to get the other person to tell you why they did not say hello.

Interestingly, the other person could have broken the silence with a socially acceptable body movement. If you shout hello to someone and that person fails to answer, BUT waves with their hand, you accept that. End of speculation. You realize that the wave answered your hello and you move on.

Focus on the speculation for one more second. Notice the control you were under by the other person. Her inaction, her silence controlled your thoughts for a noticeable amount of time. For some people, the speculation can go on for weeks and months. Sadly, some will even speculate on a single incident like that for years.

Turn it around, what if it was you that failed to acknowledge the other person. You might not even recall it, but you can be sure that the other person did. Human beings are not only physically similar, but we all think alike in many ways.

Think of a recent conversation that you had with someone. There must have been a moment when the other person gave you some indication that they were paying attention to you. It might have been an "Uh-huh," a nod, or some other verbal or non-verbal signal to indicate that a connection was still intact between the listener and the speaker.

I remember a game we used to play in a behavioral psychology course in college where you could guide a conversation into whatever your direction you wanted by the judicious use of "uh-huh." People will continue to speak on whatever subject you want as long as they perceive that they have a connection with the listener.

All that stops when the listener no longer acknowledges the speaker. When these signals wane or stop, the conversation also grinds to a halt. Try it. The next time someone starts talking to you about anything at all, just play silent. You will find that the speaker, receiving no queues from you that you are interested, will either change the topic or leave you alone. That is, if you can be silent long enough.

One of the interesting phenomena about being a silent listener is that it is uncomfortable for you as well. Try going to a business networking meeting and walk around without saying anything to anyone who approaches you. What you will notice is that the conversation has not ceased, but has gone internal. You begin talking to yourself in your own head.

You might start out confidently with your experiment, but sooner or later, the inner conversation begins to focus on what the other people are thinking about you. They must think I am unsociable. I wonder if they think I cannot speak. Maybe they think I cannot speak their language. They must think I am nuts.

They might. By not opening up to an incoming speaker, it is likely that they did not open up to you. You really don't know what they are thinking. At least that is true conversationally. We will reconsider this point when we compare it to a negotiation later.

In the meantime, your internal questions mount. Since you don't know exactly what they are thinking, your mind begins to increase its speculation. The urge builds to open your mouth and say something.

This is why silence is truly uncomfortable. For silence does not eliminate the dialogue, it moves it inside where you begin to speak to yourself. You lose the insight into what the other person is thinking and begin to speculate, in a conversation with yourself, about what is in their mind.

If you can recognize this transfer of an external dialogue to an internal one, you can change this internal dialogue into a more productive one. One where you can speculate wisely, but we will cover that later.

Regardless, I left you hanging in silence with the urge to speak. Well, if the urge is now uncontrollable do it. Speak! Open your mouth! Dispel the suspicions and the speculations!

You can talk. You can talk well. You are not only sane, but clever and sophisticated. You can set the record straight just by speaking. You know the right words to state your position, make your case, and impress your listener. Your clever speech will set the record straight.

Before you speak, though, think of what Abraham Lincoln once said:

"Better to remain silent and be thought stupid than to speak and remove all doubt."

Not only is this a vote for silence, but the quote identifies the second reason people avoid silence even if they can handle the discomfort. The fear of being stupid.

This fear is what forces many people from the power of silence into the powerlessness of noise. One never knows, but this primal fear may have caused the birth of the "uh-huh."

We have all run into a situation where we have responded to someone in a conversation when a response was not necessary, just to make sure that they thought we were following along—that we were not stupid.

"You DO know, don't you?"

How often have you uttered a tentative "Sure." when you really were not sure? Seemingly, it is better to risk the embarrassment of someone finding out that you were not sure than to be though of as not following along. Discomfort, fear of being stupid, and fear of embarrassment, with company like that is it any wonder that we avoid silence in communicating with others?

But what about the other guy?

We know why you avoid silence, but the other guy will avoid it as well for all of the same reasons. This is why silence is the most powerful negotiating technique you can master.

When you are silent in a negotiation, the other guy begins his internal conversation. The fears begin to mount for him. He begins to question your intentions. Have you offered all you can? Are you thinking his product or service is not worth it? Don't you like me? Don't laugh, all of the questions that mount in you when someone is not telling you their thoughts, mount in the other guy as well. He's got to know what you are really thinking and the only way is to get you to speak. So what does he do? He speaks first.

How do you feel now? Powerful, that's how.

Silence keeps the other person guessing

The questions only continue the more you keep your thoughts to yourself. Surprisingly, you will find that the dialog has little to do with your inadequacies but with his. Thoughts like "Am I making myself clear?" "Am I winning or am I losing?" run through the sellers head. These thoughts clearly leave you in control. You know your objective. You know what you want. It is the other person who is guessing.

Some of my most successful negotiations have begun by me stating my objective and then just shutting up. I have even used this technique on the phone. You might think that a salesperson on the phone will hang up on you if you are too quiet, but you will find that their professional courtesy stops them. Besides, they need to sell to live. Silence is just something else they have to deal with.

Needless to day, it is often easier to achieve success when this technique is used in person. Here's an example of how you can use silence to your advantage.

> You: "I would like to buy this television please?
> Salesperson: "Yes sir, we have it on special today for $250.00."
> You: "$250?" (This must be asked as a question)

At this point the salesperson will probably explain why $250 is a great deal. Just listen in silence and look interested, but not overly so. From this point on, every comment from you MUST be practically dragged out of you. If you seem interested but do not give the salesman any signals that he is getting through, he is the one who usually gets somewhat uncomfortable. He will keep trying to justify the price, but if he does not seem to be getting through, he just might say:

"If you buy it now, I might be able to give it to you for $240."

At this point, your silence is winning the negotiation. He is now on a mission to convince you to purchase it from him, and your silence is making him wonder why you haven't bought it yet. You will probably feel uncomfortable when you try this first, but this technique will save you money. It has for me many times. There are other techniques that can also be applied at this point and we will cover them later in the book. Just notice that silence, by itself, can achieve your goal.

If you want to ask or say anything, you can ask if you can get it less than $240. If you feel that you need to talk about something, call a friend after this experience. In the meantime, give the salesperson as little information about your needs and wants as possible.

If you feel stupid or embarrassed or if the seller makes you feel that you just don't know what he is talking about, just smile. If you get the television for $200, does it matter if the salesperson thinks you are stupid? Anymore stupid customers like you and he will need to take up a new line of work.

As with all negotiation tools, the key to using silence effectively is the timing of its use. The best time to use silence is after you have made your request or stated your demand. Give the request or demand sometime to be taken in and understood. Remember, if you are asking the person to reduce the price on something, you have to give them a chance to see if they can do it. Don't expect immediate responses. Become accustomed to waiting quietly for a response.

And when their response is given, give yourself a little quiet time to consider it fully. Sometimes, this silent interlude is broken by the other party offering an additional concession. Remember, your silence now is making the other side wonder if their offer was adequate enough. They just might panic and think they need to add some more to make it acceptable to you.

One of the other benefits you gain by closing your mouth is that it magically opens your ears. You might just hear something that you can use to your profit. Listening becomes an active skill versus a passive one. Use your quiet time to clearly hear and recognize what the other party is saying. Develop your powers of observation to not only hear what the other person is saying, but recognize their body language and the messages they are sending you.

Just don't forget your own body language. Don't let your eyes scream, "I want it!" while you are keeping your mouth shut. If you can learn to control your mouth and your other bodily movements, you can control the negotiation. Control equals power. That is why silence is one of the most powerful negotiating tools you have.

9

Succeed with a Great Plan

If I took you outside, threw a football at you, and said let's play, you would probably just do it. Most likely, we would begin by throwing the ball back and forth. Let's say we meet a few friends and invite them to join in. We might even organize a small game between two "teams." Some people call this a "pick-up" game. The game has a simple objective—to win the game by scoring a few touchdowns (getting the ball past a certain point on the field).

Even if football is not your game, you can most likely recall a game of some sort that you began in a similar fashion. Regardless of what the game was, you usually knew the immediate objective—to score some points—and the final objective—to win the game. Once again, the game and the objective were simple.

Buying and selling is just another game that, for the most part, begins just as casually. Shopping is a game that millions play everyday. Most people find shopping fun exactly because it seems like play. It is a game where people use their points (dollars, credit, etc.) to win something (the item they purchase—the objective). The easier the game, the more fun people have.

Remember my friend from the introduction who bought the new Toyota. He walked into the Toyota dealer, looked at the price tag, and gave the dealer his money. No negotiation, no trouble. He knew his objective, the car, and he had the credit rating to get it. What an easy way to win!

Easy, if you are willing to spend thousands of dollars more than you have to. For the seller, it was not only an easy game but a very, very profitable one. While the buyer was happy with the car, I am sure he would have been much happier if he saved the money. The lesson is simple. Buying a car is not a pick-up game.

Let's go back to our pick-up football game. You would not think twice of beginning the game like I described above, but what if I told you that I had the defensive line of the New York Giants outside and that we were going to have a game with them. Care to play now? If you didn't faint right away, you would probably want to know how I thought we stood a chance against them.

Why? It's just a game. The objectives are the same—score points and win the game. The reality is that now we are beginning a game where the chances of getting killed have risen above the potential chance of winning. We have moved from a simple, pick up game to a game played against professionals. You need to have more talent if you are going to play against a squad of professionals. These people eat, sleep, and drink football. They know all of the rules, the strategies, and tactics that win a football game. If all you know is a simple objective, how do you intend to get past those who have been studying the game their whole life and know all the possibilities?

Shopping is a game that is played by both amateurs and professionals. Those Toyota dealers, and any car dealer for that matter, are clearly professionals. They spend their lives learning about their product, about the sales practice, and, in the process, all about the amateurs that arrive on their doorstep. An amateur buyer, going up against an experienced car dealer, is as likely to win both the car AND the best price as the amateur footballer will win against the Giant's defensive line. It's not going to happen.

If you are going to meet the professional sellers, you are going to have to learn how to play the game of shopping like a professional. Just like the professionals you are going to have to build a plan to win. You are going to have to become a professional buyer.

Your overall plan, as a professional buyer, does not always have to be elaborate. Obviously if you are spending a lot of money for something, it will be worth your time to write down a plan and carefully execute it. With practice, though a plan can become something very simple. Whether simple or complex, the elements of the plan can be summarized into three steps:

1. Define your objective.

2. Develop your plan.

3. Take action!

Let's do this by example. Say you want to buy a high priced stereo system.

Step 1. Define your objective

Obviously, the initial goal is to buy the stereo system, but you need to do a little more work to truly define your objective. Follow these simple steps to help you define your objective for this purchase:

1. Do some research—Who makes stereo systems? Which ones do you like? Which do the experts recommend (consult the library, magazines, the internet, etc)? What features do they have? Which must you have? Which are unimportant? How much are you willing to pay for the one you want? (It is important to find the one you want <u>first</u> before you handle the price. You might be able to get the one you really want for less through negotiation. Too many people start with the amount they have to spend, and then buy what they think they can afford. It is better to get the best for less than get the affordable, but lesser quality product.)

2. Make a list—Take the results of your research and compile a list of the systems you want to explore. Isolate the important issues related to the purchase. Review chapter five for ideas on potential considerations and tradeoffs involved in the purchase. Turn each choice into a package of features and all potential considerations. Know what package you want to buy and the parts you can trade off in the negotiation.

3. Research possible dealers—Who sells this kind of system? Who charges the most and who charges the least and why? Make a list and rank the dealers from low price to high. Prepare to call on the ones who give you the lowest price and deliver the package you want.

You should now be able to state a clearly defined objective. Instead of just a goal like "buying a stereo system," your new objective might look something like this:

I intend to buy a (manufacturer #1) stereo system with (manufacturer #1) speakers for $650.00. This is the maximum I will pay. It must have the following features: A, B, C. I will only consider spending a little more if the dealer includes features D, E, and F. In fact, I will try to get the dealer to include them within my maximum spending limit. The standard warrantee is sufficient.

By taking the time to do the research and clearly define your objective, you build strength that will help you when you meet the dealer. For example, if the dealer tries to switch you to a higher margin (for him) system, you can explain to him why you want the manufacturer #1 system. If he tries to meet your price without feature C, you can explain why this will not do. If he tries to sell you an extended warrantee, you can explain why you don't need it.

The dealer might not do any of these things, but then again he might. I once had a computer dealer try to sell me an extended warrantee by telling me that a certain component was not covered under the existing standard warrantee. I knew better because I had done my research.

Now, obviously, this might be a little too much work for a small purchase, but the amount of work you do is up to you. I recommend trying this out on a small purchase, just to give you the practice. Practice will help make the work easier when you really need to employ this technique.

Step 2. Develop your plan

Once you have your objective clearly defined, use your research and your list to develop your plan for getting all the things you want.

For example, your plan could be very simple. You will start contacting the dealers on your list. If the first dealer meets your objective, you are done. If not, you should include in your plan what you will do next.

Now let's assume that your research has produced a number of potential dealers for the system you want. Find the dealer that is most convenient for you and put him on the top of your list. Then list the next most convenient, and so on. Determine, how far into the list you will go before doubling back to see if you can negotiate with the earlier dealers. Perhaps your plan will be to concentrate on the first dealer exclusively. These are all decisions to make in developing your plan. Just understand this concept, if you know where you plan to go you will probably get there.

Too many people, just shop without any preconceived notion of what they want and what they are willing to pay. Sellers call these people "impulse buyers." They often produce the most profits for the sellers. When people buy "on impulse," they throw away thoughts of saving money or negotiation to the wind.

The next time you are at the supermarket, look at the shelves around the checkout. Notice the candy bars and newspapers. These are targeted at the impulse buyer. You are standing there waiting for your turn at checking out your groceries and there is a newspaper with a headline that is just too tempting to pick up and read. Maybe you are hungry and, lo and behold, there is a candy bar! Supermarkets sell lots of papers and candy this way.

For candy and newspapers, I am willing to buy on impulse. For a big ticket item, I want to know I am getting what I want at the price I want. Build a plan.

As I mentioned, it does not have to be complicated. If I were negotiating over a transistor radio for under a hundred dollars, I would probably build my plan within fifteen minutes in my head. If I were looking to get that car or an expensive sofa, I might take the time to just sketch out a plan on a piece of paper.

The trick to planning a proper strategy is to know when you should take the time to plan in detail, or when the back of an envelope or even just moments thought will do.

In general, if you are really concerned about the success of the negotiation, take some more time to plan. Just remember that your time is valuable as well. Some people take so much time in planning that they never take any action on the plan. Don't be one of them.

Step 3. Take action!

Step three is self explanatory. You must take action on your plan. Before you take any action, though, you will need to make sure that you have an adequate number of negotiation techniques to win. You already have learned the essential techniques up to this point.

You have learned to put fear aside. You have learned to ask. You have learned the importance of keeping your mouth shut. Many times, these techniques will be enough, but before you visit that first dealer, you can use a few more. We will review in depth the techniques we have covered so far, and add some additional ones to make you an even better negotiator. You are getting closer to the point where you will not only keep their hands out of your pocket, but also get the items you want for less.

10

Master these Negotiation Techniques to Win

Techniques are the actions you take when you negotiate. This is where your purchase plan meets the road. It is no accident that we took so long to get to this point. While negotiation techniques are important, they should always be used within the context of a plan. You might just apply one of these techniques on a simple, small purchase, but it would be a mistake to try it on something of importance.

If you try one of these techniques on something complicated and you fail, where do you go next?

Most people know that the objective in a basketball game is to score goals to get the most points to win. Everyone who plays the game knows the techniques used in running, dribbling, and passing the ball. The only problem is the defense put up by the other team. They also know all the techniques. They also know ways to disrupt them. They have their own plan that they use to play against you.

When you go out to buy something, you are going against the defense of the seller. Some sellers, like car dealers, have gone through training session after training session on selling skills. You can bet that at least one session is dedicated to negotiation techniques to use against buyers. Just about every negotiation technique in all of the books ever written is covered.

In addition, they have honed and sharpened every skill they know to get you to buy at the price or at the feature set they want to sell. A careless use of a buyer's negotiation technique on your part can be slapped down immediately. Without a good plan on your part, you may not know where else to go.

Even if the salesman hasn't received formal training, he has learned what to do by selling to others before you walked into the showroom. Most sellers of anything have seen hundreds of people like you. They have probably had at least one person try the technique you will employ. They might have lost to it the first time it was used on them, but they probably said to themselves that they would not let that happen again. In fact they might even be waiting for someone like you to come in and try to use that negotiation technique. You have been set up.

You might be thinking, if these people know all the techniques already, what chance do I have?

Let's go back to the basketball example. In all the years that people have been playing basketball, the basic techniques of the game have remained relatively the same. People run and pass to get the ball down the court and the other side will try to take the ball away and prevent you from scoring a goal. Everyone knows the techniques, but no one knows your strategy for deploying them. The winners learn to use the right techniques at the right time.

If you just willy-nilly use the negotiation techniques that we will discuss, your chance for success will depend on the defense you will meet. If they have never heard of them or fail to recognize their use, you will succeed. If they know what you are doing and if they are experienced in meeting your technique, you will lose and have no where else to go.

That is why it is so important to learn more than just negotiation techniques to succeed. You need to recognize and address your fears. You need to understand the importance of winning twice. You need to understand the value in what you are negotiating for and the traps that the professionals set for you. You need to plan.

Now you are ready to master some useful negotiation techniques to make you a strong negotiator. Some of these will be familiar. Don't skip over the ones you have seen before. Read them again to make them solidly stick in your consciousness.

Watch a professional basketball game. The stars of the game just fly down the court. You know they are not thinking about how they are bouncing the ball or where they need to stop to make the shot. They operate on automatic. Their muscles have learned to react without thinking, to perform the actions that make the goal.

A solid plan will give you an edge, but when you take action anything can happen. You must learn these techniques so you can enter any negotiation without thinking about them. You must learn to apply them automatically as necessary. That is how the professionals do it. You must now lose your amateur status.

Ready, set, go!

Technique 1—Ask for a lower price

This may seem too obvious and familiar, but many people are afraid to ask why something costs a specific amount.

Asking a question like "Why is it so expensive?" is so simple, and yet many people are afraid to ask it. Once you ask, the seller can respond in a number of ways. He can react with surprise and shock and wait to see what you say next. More likely, he will explain why the product or service is priced at the price point he gave you. Sometimes, he will just give you a discount on the spot.

If the seller responds immediately with a discount, you might probe against this. It might indicate a willingness to negotiate further. Then again, he might just blurt out exactly the price you want to pay. Just remember to check to see that the blue bird is real. Sometimes a seller will want to get the product sold quickly to disguise a defect. If you are sure that you are getting what you want at the quality you want, do not be afraid to take advantage of a quick move on the part of the seller. Then again, there is no harm in probing to see if this is his lowest price.

It is often helpful to test whether the seller is following a "rule of three." I have known sellers who always gave their best price as their third price. Ask one time, and you got the first price. Once more and you got the second price, but ask the third time and he gave you his final price.

These sellers think that many buyers need an extra push to buy, and play this game of three's to satisfy the buyer's craving for a lower price. They mechanically group their prices into three categories. One price is for the shy, who pay the highest price just because they don't ask. The next is for those who need to be pushed a little to make up their minds. Finally, the last is for those hard to close. If you notice this is the seller's modus operendi, don't disappoint him, hold out for the third price.

Along the way to that third price, you will find that the seller will move back a step and explain why his product is definitely worth his stated price—even if he has moved that price for you already.

Many sellers are insecure about what they are selling and need to remind themselves, let alone you, why their offering is as valuable as the price they are asking. Your reticence to buy is based upon what they think are your "objections." Salespeople for major products and services receive extensive training on identifying your potential objections and their best tactics for overcoming them.

This is your chance to learn both about the seller and all of the reasons he values the object that he is selling. In addition, it gives the seller a chance to voice what he thinks are your objections and the reasons he thinks you can do away with them and buy. Think and make careful notes about each point that he says makes the product or service valuable. Carefully watch the way he identifies the objections that he thinks you have and why they are immaterial. He has chosen these points and raised the potential objections because he thinks that these are the points that are spinning around in your mind, not his.

For example, if he says that his product has gold fixtures it is because he thinks you will be impressed and will trade your hard-earned money for those gold fixtures. He might even raise a potential objection about serviceability—referring to his extensive warrantee (Note the pattern:

potential objection = his solution). Each note you make now can turn to savings later.

For you will use these exact same points to SUBTRACT some value from his offering. We will cover this idea more in technique number four.

In the meantime, there is always the possibility that the seller will react with surprise and shock that you had the gall to question his price. Depending on the amount of reaction, he can drive you to real embarrassment, that you had the nerve—let alone the audacity—to question his price. Even if he has made you feel that you should never have crawled out from under a rock into his place, you should stand your ground calmly. Take a slow, deep breath and then...

Ask the question again.

No, you are not becoming a glutton for punishment. You are just trying to determine if he knows his tactics as well as you.

Technique 2—React with surprise

There is nothing stopping you from reacting with surprise and shock as well. Although the salesperson will suffer no compunction by doing the same to you, most people will still not use this useful and rewarding tactic.

Go to a major auction gallery and listen to some of the conversations. A few years ago, I attended the pre-sale exhibition of some modern art at the New York branch of a major auction house. I mentioned to my wife that I had seen something that looked like a brush from a car wash hanging on the wall.

There was another couple looking at it when I took her to see it. The gentleman asked the nearest auctioneer how much it was expected to fetch. "$15,000," was the answer. "Oh," gentleman replied as if he had already expected it to cost that much.

Thanks to the pressure of my wife's hand on my arm dragging me quickly away, we avoided the scene of me screaming at the top of my lungs, "15,000!!!"

I am sure the other man really felt the way I did, but he carefully controlled his reaction.

Why? He let the auction house tell him what it was worth. After all, if this major auction house—an arbiter of the international art world—thought it was worth that much, it must be. If he reacted like I wanted to, they might think him uneducated, uncouth, and verifiably stupid about the art market. To save such embarrassment, he had decided to react with disinterested, appreciation of the price—like he also was an art connoisseur.

In fact, he was not. I only wish I got his card so I could show him a car wash brush or two for about two thousand less. He did walk away, though, free of embarrassment.

Don't be afraid to be embarrassed. There is nothing stopping you from reacting to a price with surprise and shock. After all, many a salesperson thinks that he needs to educate you to buy his product. He is already assuming you are stupid with regard to his offering, why disappoint him.

Ahh, you are thinking, I don't want him to think I am a tyro. I don't want to have him think me a mere country bumpkin against his city-folk sophistication. Why identify myself as a sheep to this wolf?

Well, you may be a sheep, but you are a sheep with an education. An educated sheep can beat the wolf, especially if the wolf doesn't see you coming. Let the wolf think he has the advantage and he will explain to you all you need to win. Be confident. At the very least, it's good to find out early how much of a wolf you are facing. I certainly would want to know this salient fact about the other guy. If I know that this seller has designs on my jugular, I might want to choose a different seller to deal with.

Don't be afraid to drop your defenses early, before the other person even recognizes they are down. There is no reason why you cannot raise them later when the other person no longer expects them to be there.

The risk of embarrassment is not only overstated, but used very profitably by sophisticated sellers. That is why many a seller would not think twice about indicating that your questions are naïve.

If it is good enough for the seller, it is good enough for the buyer. Take the risk and, when the opportunity is there, feel free to react with surprise at what the seller is offering.

Technique 3—Be very quiet

Once you ask your questions, once you react, once you take any action whatsoever, wait in silence for the reaction of the other party. If it takes five minutes wait for a reaction or some kind of statement before you move a muscle. We talked about this in chapter eight. Now it is time to memorize this concept and make it a part of your nature.

When a salesperson is talking, you should listen carefully for all of the needed queues and information as indicated in technique number one. In addition, each moment of silence on your part, indicates to the salesperson that you are, at the very least, thinking about his pitch and, at the most, becoming unreadable. This is a useful technique even if you seem to be already getting everything you want.

There is a great episode of the TV show *Seinfeld* where Kramer has spilled coffee and burned himself at a coffee boutique. He sues the parent of the boutique chain for the injury the hot coffee caused on his leg. The audience sees the chairman of the chain talking in a closed meeting to his lawyers and agreeing with them that he will offer Kramer free coffee for life and $50,000.

In the meantime, Kramer, whose burn has miraculously healed, is scared that the other party will find out his injury was not as bad as it was. He runs into the chairman's office with his lawyer and, as the chairman starts to tell him their offer, interrupts him at the offer of free coffee and accepts it—never hearing about the $50,000 part of the offer. That was a win/win negotiation with a twist. The chairman was happy to save the $50,000 and Kramer was happy with free coffee for life. The twist was that Kramer's lack of patience, and failure to listen quietly to the complete offer, cost him $50,000.

There are many cases where speaking to soon, or just not staying tightlipped long enough, has caused people to lose out on opportunity or worse.

I once received a free cassette player by using nothing more than this technique of being quiet. I had ordered a set of literary tapes from a vendor who, two weeks after my order was placed, had begun offering a free cassette tape player for new subscribers. When I saw the new advertisement, I called and asked for my tape player. Their agent apologized and said that this was a new offer and it did not apply two weeks ago when I had ordered my tapes.

Rather than just hang up disappointed, I just calmly repeated my request and asked him if he felt that was fair. Once he repeated to me his answer, I just stayed their on the line without saying anything.

If you tried the experiment I suggested in chapter eight, you know what happens when you leave someone in silence on the phone. Both sides want to break the silence. I left it up to him. After a few seconds, he asked if I was still there. I said yes, and then said nothing. He then began talking about why he couldn't. He could still hear me breathing, and he knew that I was still not going to hang up. Finally, he said that he understood my frustration. I still said nothing. Then he said that he would check with his supervisor to see if he could do anything. Still, I was quiet. He came back on line and said I was lucky, they would send me the tape player.

Luck had nothing to do with it. I just stood my ground and said only the words that were important, "how do I get my free tape player?" Once you state your position, give the other party a chance to give it to you. Wait before you make your next move. Don't be rushed into speaking too soon. Be quiet as long as you can.

Technique 4—Devalue the offering

No matter how much you want something, no matter how valuable the world considers the object of your desires, there is always something that is negative about it. You might be happy to accept a ton of gold, until I ask you where you want me to put it. Most likely, you will ask me to wait until you can consider your storage options. Having it might be a blessing, but putting it someplace and keeping it there might be a problem.

This is only one of the tarnishing aspects of gold. There are many other considerations. Did I mention the whole ton was in a single cube? Of course, you have a forklift to move it, don't you? Perhaps, it might be more manageable if I instead give it to you in many, many bags of coins. Would it?

Something negative can be found in everything. Each negative characteristic that you find should reduce the value to you in some way, shape, or form. Perhaps, that is the best way to look at this technique. Consider what the value of the product or service is to YOU, not to anyone else, but to you. Then look for all of the negative aspects for having it and use these in the negotiation.

Review the chapter on what something is worth. Remember, the story about my mother and the tree removal in the introduction. Because the tree service said that it cost $4,500 to remove the tree, the value of their service was $4,500. How were we able to get it done at $1,500 then?

We devalued the offering. No matter how big they said the tree was, I focused on the fact that it was a just a single tree. It sounded so simple to me. No matter how much they embellished the work they were going to do, she could not afford to spend that much money. I told her to keep checking with tree services until she reached someone who understood our position instead of selling us on theirs.

We focused on what we wanted to spend, not what they wanted to charge. As it is with most services, there is always someone who will do it for less. The main issue is finding someone who will charge less, but do it reliably. We shopped until we found that person.

Well trained salespeople don't worry about the price of what they are selling, even if you cannot afford it. They will not only enhance the value of their offering, but often find the means, potentially through financing, for you to pay for it. In the case of a credit offering, you can keep paying for it.

In the research phase, you should identify what your limit is for your expenditure. As I mentioned in the first technique, a talkative and educated seller will work to present you with all of the reasons why his product or service is worth the asking price. As you note these, you will need to counter his benefits by finding ways of subtracting value from his offering.

Obviously, if you show him reasons why his offering is less valuable, he should be able to reduce his asking price to you.

For example, when I purchased the floor model VCR, I countered the salesman's arguments about the unit's top-of-the-line status, with the fact that it appeared it had a lot of dust on it from being out on the shelf. Regardless of its notable features, the feature that I expressed concern about was the dust. He knew that I was not going to pay top dollar due to my perceived concept of its current condition.

You might even review a thesaurus before going to the store to prepare your brain with antonyms (opposite words) to use when discussing the item with the salesperson.

The product is in a beautiful metal case; you say you wanted wood. The finish is a high gloss; you say you wanted matte. It's very appealing; you say that you wanted something less attractive.

You need to find something to subtract from the seller's offering to make it easier for the salesperson to compromise on price. Obviously if it is less valuable to you, you will need and want to spend less money on it.

Don't think this technique is too aggressive. Keep in mind that a good salesman has already been trained by experience or educated in salesmanship to recognize your objections and to counter them. You need to take a moment to train your responses to counter his counter-objections. If properly applied, the concessions you achieve were most likely even considered in advance by the seller.

If this is true, you might be thinking why he didn't give you the lowest price to begin with. Why should he? If he can get more for each purchase, he grows his business. He gets more money for the things he wants. Sometimes he will meet someone like you who will want to negotiate, and he needs to have some room to maneuver. More often than not he will meet those who will pay his price right off the bat. His business is built on striking a balance between those who want to negotiate and those who will not.

Do not let any seller convince you that he is losing money on your sale. Keep in mind that he also has the right to walk away from any deal that he does not like. If he is taking your money, you can safely assume that he has found some way to profit from your purchase—even if it is only unloading the merchandise.

One last point on subtracting value, it is your job to reduce the value of something not the sellers. Smart sellers will also use a variation on this technique to get the pricing you want. "Yes, I can sell you the car that you want at your price, if we remove the radio. Maybe this is acceptable to you, but for me I don't want a hole in my dashboard for the former radio.

Like winter follows fall, his next remark will be along the lines of. "Well, I would like to meet your price, but you see I need to remove something to do it." This is a very good negotiator, if he notices you are willing to remove value for the price then he will help you.

If you get into this situation, don't run and hide. Just look for a chance to agree. Find something of value that is immaterial to you and remove that—not his selection but yours. This is all part of the game. If you are going to play you have to be prepared for this. Do not let the seller subtract value from your purchase that's your job.

Be prepared for another value game the seller may try. When discussing value you need to concentrate carefully. I recently went with a relative to a car dealer and told him that the most we could spend for a particular car was $14,000. He wanted $14,500. I restated our position and he went to talk to his manager. When he came back, he said the manager agreed. I was happy. He then said that the only issue was that we would have to pay the "destination charge." How much was that? It was $500.

Wait a minute. $14,000 plus $500 equals $14,500. Isn't that what I just refused? No, he said, he met my price. I just failed to add the destination charge. My relative even asked if everyone pays this charge and the dealer said yes. I reviewed with him my math abilities and said I disagree. $14,500 equals $14,500 whichever way you look at it. I told him I appreciated his time and we left.

At a different dealership, we purchased the car for $13,700. My relative asked me again if we paid the destination charge. I laughed. The fact of the matter is that I don't care if we did or didn't. Car dealers will piece together the parts of the deal anyway they want to get the price they want. Your job is to make sure you get all the pieces you want at the price you want to pay

Technique 5—Use a partner—real or invisible

In the last example, I went with a relative to the car dealership. It is a good idea to always have two people on your side whenever you go to negotiate anything. Two heads are better than one, as the saying goes.

One of the best techniques you can use within a negotiation is to bring in a partner who will be on your side to help you get the most from a transaction. It is no longer you against them, but your team against theirs. You have more power when you can bring in more talent to help you and you can do so—even if your team or that partner is invisible.

Your partner should be the one who ideally has all the reasons for NOT buying. In fact, it would be helpful for your partner to put up more resistance that you can muster yourself. He or she is the bad guy/ gal that is keeping you from making the purchase decision. That is why this negotiation concept of a using partner is often called the good guy/ bad guy technique.

The good guy/bad guy technique gets its name from the practice used in many prisoner interrogations. Many film noir classics have examples of this technique where a physically threatening interrogator is just about to strike the suspect of a crime. All of a sudden, a good guy grabs the arm of the "bad guy," and suggests he leave the room and cool off.

Once the tough interrogator has left the room, the "nice" interrogator, gives the suspect a cigarette, and tries a more reasonable approach. He explains how truly crazy and unpredictable the other interrogator is, and how the suspect should seriously consider coming clean by confessing to him, the "good guy."

The hope of the interrogation team is that, in his fear and confusion, the suspect will forget that both people are working in concert to get what they want out of him. If he won't succumb to the threatening maniac, he might just open up to the more reasonable approach knowing that he can save himself a lot of physical discomfort. Only the masochistic, opt to go back to the maniac. Like the old saw, "you can attract more flies with honey than you can with vinegar." The sugary approach often wins the confession.

From under the bright lights of an intense interrogation, this technique has moved out into the daylight of the real commerce.

Car dealers are the most notorious for employing this tactic. No matter how successful you have been in negotiating with the salesman, invariably he will tell you that in order to get approval he will need to bring your offer into his manager's office. Your salesman has now become the "good guy" and the manager has been identified as the "bad guy."

In nine times out of ten, he will emerge from the manager's office with the dire report that, while he felt your position was very reasonable, his manager—the bad guy—needs to either ask for more money, change the terms, or find some other concession from you.

Of course, your friend, the good guy salesman, will do all he can to help you, but you have to help him by working on further concessions.

What should be patently obvious to you is that both people work for the dealership and neither is looking to build a long-term loving relationship with you. Both people are committed to find a way to sell you the car, but the salesman will build on his good guy image for two reasons. First, he may be successful in convincing you to team with him against his manager (of course, it may not be fully to your own interest) and second, if he fails, he can always be the "guy who was on your side."

This may seem unimportant now, but he leaves you a positive resource for you to employ in the future. From childhood on, many people have difficulty going back to someone who tells them no. This salesman, however, never really said no to you. It was his manager, the bad guy. By using this tactic, you believe the salesman is still on your side and you will be comfortable going back to him. Even if you don't, you can be sure that he will feel free to contact you in the future. After all, he was your friend, the good guy.

This good guy/bad guy tactic is successfully used all the time by the seller against the buyer. Now you can use the same technique as the buyer.

First, it should be clear to you that you are the good guy. You are the one who is willing to spend the money to get what you want. Yes, you can be the seller's friend as well.

You want what he has and you are willing to pay, but there is another party who will influence your decision—the bad guy.

Don't go looking for some threatening monster. You already have the person who will play the role. You have a friend, a spouse, or even someone who is totally unrelated to you. For example, another dealer can take the form of the bad guy. The bad guy does not even have to be present. The person is not bad in the sense of evil. The person is considered "bad" for the seller since he, she or it is the one who will prevent you from buying.

If you have someone who can accompany you when you go to the store, take advantage of it. If I am shopping for something expensive for the home, I will bring my wife.

Before we leave the house, however, we discuss the purchase and review a few signals that we will use to communicate strictly between ourselves. For example, we determine that she will shake her head back and forth, a typical signal that means "no," if she really thinks we should get it. In addition, we coach each other to suggest opposing views on the item we are going to see.

When we were planning our first home together, we went to a store to purchase a mattress. I had wanted to get a top-of-the-line, pillow-top mattress which the dealer indicated cost about $1.500. My wife shook her head "no." In the meantime, I started looking at some others, that I personally didn't want, with the salesman who was keen to show me them since he had seen my wife's signal. Importantly, he did not know what the signal really meant.

While we were examining the other mattresses, I told the dealer that I really wanted the pillow top, but my wife felt it was too expensive. He told me that the lowest price he could offer was $1,200. Already, her head shake had saved us $300. We were not there yet.

I told him that I thought that it was still too much. He said that he might be able to get it for us for about $1,000. This said a lot about the earlier "lowest price." I went over to talk with her, clearly out of earshot of the dealer.

I told her that we were headed in the right direction, but that I needed her to be more negative. She listened and continued to shake her head. All the time I knew that, even though we could not be heard, her body language was unmistakable. I continued to look around and then I approached the dealer. I told him that I would have bought it right on the spot, but that my wife still thought it too expensive.

He commiserated. He told me he would talk to his manager. A moment later he came back with a price of $800. This is what we paid. Her head shakes saved us $700.

By carefully choreographing this interaction between me the "good guy" and my wife the "bad gal," we were able to save almost half.

This tactic can even work for loners. No one knows who you know behind the scene there at the store. You can always allude to a spouse, a friend, or even a fantasy friend who must review the offer before you can go ahead with the purchase. Your invisible partner is now the party who will make or break the sale.

"I would like to buy it but I have to check with my husband at home," could be a response. Sometimes the seller will give you some concession to avoid having you leave the store. If they are really afraid that the invisible person will talk you out of it, the concession could be sizeable and get you to purchase. Don't worry, they will not feel offended if you no longer have to talk to the other person. In fact, if you end up buying, it doesn't matter.

In addition, the invisible partner can also help you politely disengage if you feel that you are under some serious sales intimidation or if you just want to check out another dealer.

"Thank you, I appreciate your offer, but I need discuss it with my friend," is a nice way to say you are not going to buy there and then. While this might provoke another offer (If so, be quiet and see what it is before leaving), you can still use it to disengage. Just make note of the best offer, and say that you are sorry but you still need to consult and leave.

Recognize that some very well trained salesmen will now try to identify if your partner is the one that they should be selling to directly. They will ask you if they can contact your partner directly. Be polite and thank them, but assure them that you will be the one who will buy, and you just need to consult with your partner to make sure that the purchase is ok with her. You are never under any obligation to disclose who your partner is to anyone.

Technique 6—Reveal only the information you need to win

Revealing too much information too quickly can hurt you. The correct tactic is to provide the seller with just the right amount of information required to get what you want—less if you are able, but never more than you have to. The main benefit of this tactic is that the seller now has to try to spend a lot of time trying to figure you out. He cannot easily cast you into the group of buyers that he respond to sales tactic one or the group that buys when sales tactic two is applied.

He is immediately concerned now about his ability to sell to you and that will move him from total confidence to wariness and fear. He will begin to fear that he cannot sell to you. When he finally does—at your price/performance targets—this tactic makes him feel that he has clearly won. Of course, so have you.

So make him feel good later, by making him work a little harder from the start.

Let's look at a few of the more common methods of discovery that most sellers use. The first, and often the most deadly, question a seller may ask is how much are you willing to pay.

Never tell a seller how much you have to spend. Never say, even if he begs you to know. Think about it. If I know you have $100 to spend, why would I want to sell you something for $80? If I am a good seller, I want that extra $20. If I am a great seller, I not only want the extra $20, but I also want you to buy another $100 on credit.

Yet many sellers persist in asking how much you want to spend, because this is a tactic that works nine times out of ten. Many buyers are only too happy to tell them right off the bat.

This is just one of the pieces of information that you should avoid telling the seller. I would also avoid mentioning your position in life, your assets, and anything that gives the seller an edge on you as a purchaser.

You would be surprised what people ask and what they easily get. Why do I have to give a car salesman my address to ask for some information on a car? Yet, if he has my name and address, he can start checking up on me and my credit rating. I have even had a dealer ask me for my social security number! Why not just give him access to my bank account!

Remember the lesson in the chapter on major sales traps; you don't even have to give your name.

The fact of the matter is that you do not have to give a salesperson any information about yourself or your circumstances. They may tell you that they need the information, and that they have rules that they must get it from you. The fact is that their rules are those that they themselves have created. They do not apply to you.

I recently purchased a lap top computer and the salesman gave me a form to fill out with my name, address, etc. I told him that I just wanted to pay for it with my credit card and leave. He stood there arguing with me that I needed to fill out the form before they could sell it to me. I told him that I just wanted to pay with my credit card.

One of the reasons that I did not want to fill out the form was that it had return policies and other items that I did not want to agree to. Rather than argue each point out, I just decided that it would be better to not fill it out.

The salesperson told me that I could not buy the computer without filling out the form. I mentioned that I purchased a monitor a month earlier and did not fill out any form and that my credit card was good. I suggested he see a manager. The manager came back with the same response.

He told me that the paperwork helped him have some assurance that I could identify myself and that I was not using a stolen credit card. I showed him a picture ID and said he could use it to make sure it was me. He finally just told his salesman to give me the computer and charge it. They are not going to let an internal rule stop the purchase, unless they are truly afraid of the risks. If you are reasonable with them, they will be reasonable with you.

Just because they tell you they need something does not mean they really need it. Does the electronic store really need my zip code to sell me some batteries? I don't think so. I never give it out to them.

You should look upon information about yourself as you would your savings or other valuables. Keep it under lock and key until you really need to take it out, and then do so carefully.

When you do release information about yourself, do it in a controlled way. Understand why they need the information before giving it out. Release only those pieces relevant to the purchase of the product.

For example, the most important piece of information on you is likely your social security number. When you apply for credit, your social security number is often requested. The seller can use it to check with credit clearinghouses to get a picture of your credit history. If you are looking to buy something on credit, you will most likely need to give them this number.

Amazingly, I have been asked for the number even when purchasing something for cash. Why? The reason is the same as in the earlier paragraph. The buyer wants to know more about me and my social security number gives them a key to open the information flow on me. The more they know about me, the more control they can exert on our negotiation.

With identity theft on the rise, this is one number that you want to keep to yourself as much as possible. If there is no clear reason or need for you to give out your social security number, don't. There are no laws that say you have to give out any information on yourself to salespeople if you do not want to.

Regardless of the reason, you will find that when you resist, they have to give in. Do you seriously think that a store will halt your purchase just because you refuse to give them some information that they have been asked to collect for their marketing department? I have yet to find someone who will refuse to sell me something because I did not give them the insignificant information they asked for.

Even in those situations where I will not be negotiating for a purchase, this refusal to disclose everything about me has led to a life relatively free from telemarketers and junk mail.

This brings us to the final caveat about releasing too much information on yourself. Understand the privacy policies of the seller to whom you grant disclosure. Make sure that that they will not use the information they have collected about you to make your life a marketing nightmare. If you are the type of person who likes to get hundreds of unsolicited solicitations, don't worry about it and they will come. If you think otherwise, make sure that you understand the vendor's privacy policies first before giving them anything.

Technique 7—Manage your emotions to your advantage

Remember the story of the boy and the nickel. If a pleading child gets the nickel, it is because his emotional ploy has gotten around your logical defenses. He has used sympathy to get what he wants.

Likewise, someone who is holding a gun on you and demanding a nickel will also get what they want. While these are two very different extremes, they are good examples to point out the usefulness of emotions in getting what you want from a negotiation. In the first example, your choice of giving away the nickel is still somewhat voluntary. In the second example, volition has flown out the door.

As a good negotiator, you won't need to resort to the second extreme and shouldn't. You will find, though, it still makes sense to understand and properly use positive emotions to get what you want. You need to reference two positions when looking to gain from a successful negotiation. Your first position is to know when to use positive emotions. The second position is to know when to leave the emotions at the door.

Emotions are best left in check right at the start of a negotiation. Like the boy negotiating with his father in the Bill Cosby story who wanted his dad to give him a nickel. The first request was unemotional and matter of fact. "Dad, can I have a nickel?" He will not make any demands or whine to engender sympathy until after a simple question fails to achieve his desired aim.

For many people, emotions are too easily worn on their sleeves. Salesmen lick their chops when they see a potential buyer reaching over the counters with excitement at the idea of buying what they are selling. Car dealerships are full of eager customers—especially that first-time buyer.

I have seen people ecstatic with excitement, go into a car showroom, and wax enthusiastically about the car right in front of them. It's the car of their dreams. In fact, they have dreamt about it each night, consecutively, since it was first announced in the press. The happiest day of their life will be the one when they drive it home. Now, put yourself into the shoes of the salesman. How difficult will it be to negotiate with this person?

Forget it; the buyer has already bought the car in his mind. "You do want to protect it with custom undercoating, don't you?" The salesman sees the options adding up in front of his eyes. Extended service contracts only follow the custom designed, chromium plated wheels. By the time the gleam grows cloudy in your eyes, the deal is done. How seriously do you think he will take your negotiation challenges? You might as well have just handed over your checkbook.

Yes, you can be excited. I am all for you achieving the happiness that you feel the new car will bring you. Just wait to display your pleasure until AFTER you have bought it. Don't give the seller an edge in the negotiations by displaying emotions that suggest that you want it very badly.

Learn to look neutral when approaching any salesperson. Even better, learn to look disappointed. "Yes, I am interested in that car, but, wow, it's soooo expensive."

Obviously, you are interested in buying that car or you wouldn't be asking about it. The problems with it, however, are making you think twice about it. Instead of being happy, be skeptical. Feel sad that the color is not exactly the color you wanted. Moan about how another model you are looking at is starting to look better than this one. This is where the "kick the tires" concept was born. If only this car was better constructed, had more options, or how about "cheaper." What a shame!

When your emotions point against his success, the dealer has to find some way to make you happy enough to buy it. Maybe he will throw in the chrome wheels or the top-of-the-line stereo to cinch the deal. Maybe he will just make it more affordable. After all, now your look of disappointment is starting to rub off on the salesman.

Amazingly, in a profession where confidence is an absolute necessity, you will find that salespeople also breed insecurity. If you are emotionally cool to his offering, maybe others will feel the same way. He cannot afford others to be uninterested in his offerings otherwise he will be looking for another job. You are a threat to his profession, unless he can show you why he is happy to be selling this product and he can make you join his happy clientele.

Give him the chance to convince you. The longer you take to show happiness, the more money you will save and the more features and options you will achieve. If you can learn to successfully manipulate your emotions, you are three-quarters of your way to being a top negotiator.

The key is to learn to use the right emotion at the right time. In the above example, an unemotional, cool approach is the way to go. Here is an example of a time when it was right to use happiness right from the start.

I once wrote a letter to an automobile manufacturer where right from the start I told them that the car was the car I had always dreamed of owning. Unfortunately, I was very hurt, disappointed, and my happiness was tarnished when it's transmission failed at 56,000 miles—6,000 miles AFTER the warrantee ran out.

After outlining my anguish in the note, I asked them if there was something they could do to restore my confidence in the car and their company. After all, how would they have felt if they were in my shoes or, as the case was, in their faulty automobile? More importantly, how many other people would hear my story of disappointment? How many others would not buy another one like it for fear of experiencing the same problem? In fact, what was their chance of enticing me with a new model someday in the future?

I never had to ask those last three questions in the note. I knew those questions would arise in their own minds. Marketers know that disappointed customers can have a much more deleterious impact on their business than any advertising can correct. Ultimately, it was word of mouth that doomed the Edsel.

Fortunately, this automobile manufacturer understood the value of keeping a good, happy customer. Within a few weeks of sending my note to them, they sent me a check for $850, representing half of the repair price. The burden of the entire repair bill of $1,700 was made more bearable with their 50% contribution. Like the boy with the nickel, sympathy helped.

Once again it was not a logical request that made the difference, but the appeal to the seller's feelings. Never overlook the emotional interests of the other party in the sale. Learn to read the emotions behind the seller. Perhaps, your sale makes his monthly quota. Maybe it will be the one that gives him that sales award that will send him and his wife on a trip to Hawaii. He might even feel altruistic that day as he gives you the bargain, because it helps make him happy. Maybe your sale just keeps him in business.

A good way to check on his emotions is just to ask him. If he is pushing you too hard, ask him how he would feel if he were you at this point. You might be surprised at the answer. A good time to ask is when it looks like you cannot proceed further in the negotiation. Then listen carefully, he might expose the issue that he thinks he is concerned about and it just might be something other than what you thought it was.

Sometimes, the answer has helped propel the negotiation in my favor. "Don't you feel it is still a little expensive?" might be answered by him with, "It's going on sale next week." While this important piece of information would never have been volunteered at the beginning of the interaction, the appeal to his feelings was enough to put it out on the table now.

Frustration, disappointment, sadness, happiness, these emotions can be a help or a hindrance in any negotiation. If you noticed, I have left off the list one emotion that we alluded to in the beginning of this discussion. That one is anger. Leave it off the table.

In the book, *The Godfather*, the author states that the Tom Hagen, Godfather's adopted son and advisor, learned the art of negotiation from him. "'Never get angry,' the Don had instructed. 'Never make a threat. Reason with people.'" This all powerful leader, who could not only make threats, but also execute them, knew that anger was the enemy of all negotiators.

Angers and threats can get people to do things, but it also plants seeds into the other party of revenge and hate. These emotions, in their simplest form, lead to win/lose negotiations. You gain nothing but more risks by making the other party lose through anger and forcing them to recognize that loss.

Even if you are convinced that the other party cannot possible hurt you in any way, anger and hate cloud your own judgment. You need to be vigilant in every negotiation for the factors that will make you successful. Anger will cause you to miss key pieces of information that will make you successful and perhaps even arm your opponent with the weapons to force you to lose. If you feel that you are becoming angry over a negotiation, get up and leave it. You do not want to make an agreement while your mind is occupied with negative emotions.

In addition, if the other party becomes angry, follow the Don's advice. Try to reason. If you cannot diffuse the anger, get up and leave. Be polite, but get away right away. If this is known tactic of this particular party just go to another seller or dealer.

Once, the manager at a car dealership quoted me a price on a specific model that I noticed on his property. I gave him the vehicle number and he told me that he could not give me the price I had requested on that car because it had a chrome package. He spent ten minutes telling me why that added so much to his cost. If I wanted that particular car, I had to pay an additional amount to cover the cost of the chrome package. He also said that if I found another car in his lot without the chrome package, he would give it to me at my price.

Imagine my surprise when I discovered that the car I had identified in the lot did not have the chrome package. I went back in the showroom and told the dealer that I took another look at the car we had originally talked about. I said that unfortunately he had made a mistake and that the car did not have the package he described. I would be glad to then get this car at the price we had agreed upon.

Thinking I had caught him in a lie (and perhaps I had), he grew angry and indignant. He told me that the price he had given me was the lowest he could go no matter what. As he grew increasingly angry, I just politely said thank you, and said that if he could ever meet my price I would still be interested. I then left.

His anger lost him a customer. I eventually got the same car from another dealer at less than the price he was willing to offer.

In the rest of the story that follows that quote from *The Godfather*, the Godfather leaves another person who angrily denies the path to reason. The author says that his opponent turned white with fear and emissaries were sent to bring the Godfather back into the room. Why?

A lot of people wrongly think that aggressive behavior and anger show that they are stronger in a negotiation. These people just don't know that when people walk out over scare tactics, their power walks out as well. The character in *The Godfather* not only lost his power by acting tough and unreasonable, but he had also insulted a person who was more powerful than himself.

In this case he also realizes, like many who let their anger take control, that he regrets his stupidity and tries to reopen the negotiation. If that angry dealer had called me back and apologized, I might have accepted his apology and bought the car if he agreed to the price. By leaving politely, I still gave both of us a chance to reopen the negotiation later. Of course, there is still the question of the questionable sales tactic that he used on me. That must also be considered in whether or not I should go though with the purchase.

Needless to say, anger and similar negative emotions do not help anyone in a negotiation. Those that resort to it leave the best to those who can learn to turn it against them or to diffuse it through reasonableness.

Never forget that while you should probe and explore the feelings of the seller, you need to keep your feelings on a "need-to-know" basis. Do not lose sight of the use of your emotional tools to help favorable influence the negotiation on your behalf.

Technique 8—Show them the money

When you go to a store to buy something, you usually can see what you are buying. For example, if you are shopping for a camera, you usually ask the salesperson to show it to you. Normally, the salesperson will show it to you and give you a demonstration. If you think about it, the salesman is at a clear advantage here since he can actively demonstrate everything that makes this particular camera worthy of the price he wants for it.

In the meantime, where's the money you intend to spend for it? Most likely, it is hiding in your wallet or hidden even further in the credit card. Yet, any salesman worth his salt is more interested in separating your money from you in exchange for his camera. You can equalize his advantage by showing him the money.

This is a technique that I find is the most helpful at a flea market. If there is one place that you can try all of your negotiation skills to gain experience it is at a flea market. Most sellers are used to taking a few minutes to negotiate for the items they are selling. They know people go to the flea market to find bargains. This is the perfect venue to try your negotiation techniques and this is the best place to try number eight.

Think of the seller's position. They want to get rid of a bunch of old stuff. They had to collect it, put it in boxes, lug it to the flea market, and then unpack it when they got there. They had to arrange it on the table, and then sit and wait for someone to take an interest. If their table has met little traffic, they are just dying to talk to anyone just to break the monotony of it all. Even if they see a lot of "potential "buyers, they are eager to see some of their cache leave that table. Remember, if they do not sell everything they brought with them, they have to repack it and truck it back home.

Nevertheless, that old camera sitting there has shot a lot of memories. While he has already replaced it, the owner still wants to get as much as he can for it. "$75.00" is his quote to you. Let's say you offer $30.00. All right, he knows he has to bring down the price a bit, so he counters, "I'll let you have it for $60.00."

Suddenly, you take out two crisp twenty dollar bills and make sure that he sees them. "I'm sorry," you say, "but I only have $40.00."

Now you have the seller's attention. He sees a camera that he really doesn't want and he sees the cash in your hand. He can decide to keep the camera, but he can see that you are ready to just hand him that money. Ever hear the expression, money talks. Well, you need to have its mouth there in the open for it to begin speaking. Often, it screams to the buyer, "Take me!" and they do.

Obviously, if you are buying a car, it is not advisable to bring a suitcase packed with $20,000, but there are other ways to show them the money. You might let the dealer know that you are ready to pay cash. If the dealer knows that you are ready to spend $20,000 for the car you are looking at, he might help you find someway for you to get to that number. Just be careful that he does not push you to another model where your $20,000 represents a $5,000 profit for him. The object, obviously, is to get the car you wanted for the amount that you have to spend—not that you are looking to just spend the money.

Even if you want to show him the money, you probably do not want to do this upfront. Perversely, you can frequently get what appears to be a better deal if you are willing to use their credit. In a major purchase, like a car, you want to know all of the facts before you finance.

What you are not privy to is that the finance company or the manufacturer may offer the dealer added incentives to steer people to the credit agreement. For example, the dealer might get a cash payment of a few hundred dollars if you sign the credit agreement. The financier will do this to earn the few thousands of interest from you over the term of the contract.

It might be worth it for you to finance the car, IF that gives you an overall cheaper price, but be careful. I said an OVERALL lower price. Figure out what you will be paying in total for the car and all of the financing. You will be surprised to see that the total costs of financing may amount to much, much more than if you paid cash up front.

Your objective is to find the lowest total cost or to find the way to afford the car you want. You may be in a cash situation where financing is your only option. If this is true, just shop for the best financing package. Beware of no cost or zero percent financing. These programs are often offered by the dealer at the list price of the vehicle.

Sometimes they are offered by the manufacturer directly, which means that they do not impact the dealer's profit. The dealer may have been able to sell the car for less and you could have still received the financing promotion. You might have paid $25,000 for a car that you could have paid $20,000 for with some negotiation.

Start with the concept that the dealer is going to look to separate you from as much money as they can, and then carefully examine all offers to insure that that does not happen.

Regardless whether you will finance or pay cash, if you can get them to focus on your ability to pay and your willingness to do so, they gain added incentive to bring the negotiation to a close. Remember, every moment that they spend in negotiation with you reduces their ability to move to another sale. If they know you are ready to spend, they have another reason to move quickly to end the negotiation.

Technique 9—Develop many ways to say no

Some people have a very difficult time saying no. You may be one of them. How many times have you answered a sales clerk, who has asked if you need any help, with the phrase "I'm just looking?" When asked if you are going to buy it, have you tried "I'll think about it?" Let's not forget the immortal, "We'll see."

Whatever you plan on seeing, "no" is the inferred answer. Why not just say "no" when you mean "no."

Well, "no" sounds absolutely final. It seems like an aggressive period at the end of a sentence. Here is a person has taken the time to explain to you all of the benefits of the product, and you nail him closed by saying "no." It is almost an insult. Forget it.

If the person is a professional salesman, you can bet that he is not insulted. He is, in fact, spurred on by the rejection. Many professional salespeople are educated in the concept that the word "no" is short way of saying "yes, but." Remember the concept of "objection handling." Sales representatives cannot bring out their stock of objection handlers, unless they first get some indication that you are going to disagree with their proposal.

But not every salesperson has gone to sales training 101. There are some people who will take your word no as an absolute stop to the sales process. If you really mean no and you want the process to stop, do not be afraid to use the word "no." You may have to use it a few times, but eventually, the seller will get the message.

If you are, however, in the midst of a serious negotiation, and you want to say "no" to a particular point, but keep your options open, learn to say "no" by saying "yes."

For example, if the salesman tells you that you should buy the product because it comes with a 5 year warrantee. You can say, "Yes, I agree that that is an attractive feature, but I still have an issue on the price." Notice what I did. I agreed with one of his points but brought him squarely back to an area where we still have a disagreement. By using the concept of "yes…but," I have defused his argument.

If this were a professional salesman, he probably has a ready argument for my disagreement. While he was waiting for me to say no, I confused him. I agreed with him. What does he do now? Not only did I agree with his argument, but I brought him back to the issue I wanted to clear up for me—the price. I am willing to agree with any point that sounds good to me as long as I do not agree to the sale until I am satisfied with my purchasing criteria.

It comes in five colors. Fine. They have the best service in the industry. Great. Their product has the best features. Outstanding. But……about that price. Using "yes, but" can help you get them back to the important issue and away from the objective handling phase. Again, you might be negotiating for something other than price. If so, then just use the same technique to get them to focus on your greatest need.

This is also a great technique to use when facing an aggressive or angry person. When someone is angry and they feel they know what is right for you, they are ready to take any rejection of their point of view as a point of escalation of their argument. If you agree with their position, how can they be angry? Usually, they don't even hear the words after the "but." They are so focused on their position, they are stumped that you were ready to agree. The "yes" is both unexpected and argument-shattering. This tactic is a great way for you to defuse an argument.

Technique 10—Give up and walk away

Regardless of how much you want something, you must be ready to say "no" and walk away. If you are not ready to give up and walk away from a negotiation, you have already lost. If I know that you must buy what I am selling, I can hold out on a variety of positions until you fold and buy it. We have talked about this many times here. This is one technique to memorize.

If you are drowning and I offer to throw you a life preserver for $10, you would be foolish and soon dead, to yell back to me, "how about $5?" You can negotiate until you hit the water, after that I know you will be a buyer at whatever I ask.

Realistically, do you need that exact car, that specific sofa, or that particular television. I know you have your heart set on that blue model, but is this the only dealer that has that car in blue? For most consumer goods, you can find the exact same model at a variety of dealers. The present dealer may have exactly what you want, but there are probably five others within driving distance that have the exact same thing.

When you find that the negotiation is going against you, disengage politely. Tell the salesperson that you appreciate all that he has done. Repeat back to him his best offer so you ensure that you have it right. When you are certain that you know where things stand, thank him. Tell him that you are sorry that you cannot agree now but hope you can find some way to do business in the future. If he is a good salesperson, he will allow you to leave without argument. If he gets angry or demanding, just review both positions, so you are also sure that he sees where things stand, and then tell him you have to go.

Reviewing where you both stand gives the other party one last chance to look for a compromise. On your part, you can use his last position as a starting point when you go to another dealer or seller as a beginning point for a negotiation.

Why start from scratch? You have already determined that someone will go to the point you are at with the first seller. That should be where you start the negotiations with another seller.

If you find that the other sellers will not go below the point you arrived at with the first seller, you might reconsider returning to the original seller. Obviously, if the market is such that you cannot go lower with anyone else, it doesn't matter who you buy it from so look to the one that is most convenient for you. In addition, go to the one who provides the most other features or services for the money.

If you do need to go back to the original seller, though, don't be afraid to do so. Sometimes, they will tell you that the offer they made at that point was just for that day. If so, you might want to use the "show them the money" tactic, this can push them to accept the earlier offer.

These are more techniques you can use to negotiate successfully. The more you focus on your negotiating skills, the more opportunities you will have to uncover more techniques you can use. Reading other books on negotiations can also give you additional ideas to use. Professionals never stop learning. Amateurs never begin. Don't be an amateur any longer.

11

Practice, Practice, Practice

There are times when you must research. There are times when you must plan and study negotiation techniques. There are times that you must just act.

When purchasing a car on any other high value item, you will obviously want to take some time and exercise some patience. A new car, for example, represents one of the largest purchases an individual will make. This is the type of purchase that cries out for all of your best negotiation skills. You will be dealing with the best negotiators in the world. If you studied this book carefully, I am sure that you will be ready to secure the best deal—as long as you have become experienced in USING your new negotiating capabilities.

Don't wait until you face the big deal to try negotiating. This sounds very obvious, but even if you bought this book to help you on that big deal, you should wait until you have tried out your skills on a small purchase a few times before trusting them for the big one.

If I gave you a golf ball, a golf club, and a few minutes of instruction on how to hit the ball, you could probably hit a couple of balls at a driving range with little or no difficulty. Your aim might be off, but at least you will know how to hit the ball. Would you even consider going up against Tiger Woods at this point? No way.

Why would you then try your first negotiations against the A-team at a car dealership? They are just as professional at negotiating as Tiger Woods is at playing golf. Before you face the best negotiators, you should build up your ability to use some of the negotiation tactics mentioned here by negotiating for smaller things. You should gain experience practicing these skills in the marketplace, but in situations where you won't get mauled.

There are lots of opportunities all around for you to try some of the techniques and strategies outlined in this book. Start with a simple test. The next time you are buying something, just wince when someone tells you the price.

For example, if you are looking for a hotel room and you are given a price of $100, just wince and say "$100?" and then shut up. Observe what the other person does. Usually this action is enough to get them to offer you something lower. If they don't, just remain silent for a long minute. If they still do not budge or begin explaining reasons why they cannot go lower, you can venture some reasons of your own why you cannot go higher.

Remember, I am assuming that you have done at least some minimal research and know that this hotel is not the only one left in town, and that it isn't booked solid with the largest convention in the neighborhood. If you find that this is one of the reasons why the hotel staff is intransigent (they just might tell you this when they explain why they cannot go lower), realize that it will be difficult if not impossible to get them to move lower.

Think about the limited edition concept. If what they have is truly scarce and if you must really have it, your chance of negotiating the price down diminishes. If this is indeed the situation, recognize it as such. Find another hotel.

If you are faced with no choice on the price, and you must get the room, see if you can get some added value. Ask if you can get an upgrade or a coupon for a free breakfast. As long as you are polite and present your wishes as questions rather than demands, most people will try to give something to make up for the fact they are unable to offer you what you originally wanted.

If you need a television or other small electronic purchase, use it as another chance to practice your new skills. If the dealer says it will be $100, say that you only wanted to spend $80. Then, shut up and wait quietly. He might show you another model or he might offer the one you are interested in for the $80. If he shows you another model, pause, thank him for finding something in your price range, and mention that you are still interested in the first.

Ask again, politely, if there is anything he can do with the price of the original model. At this point he may offer a discount or some other feature—extended warrantee for example. He might not offer the $80 price but he might go to $90. Judge if this is truly an adequate savings for you. Buy it or try to negotiate further.

If you are shopping for anything, take a moment and think if this is an opportunity to try out your new negotiation skills. Make it a game. Try to negotiate, even if it is for something that costs very little, every time you are buying something.

Just think, if you didn't even try in the above two examples, you would have paid whatever the seller asked. If you try, though, you might save ten or twenty dollars each time. That ten or twenty dollars in savings goes right back into your pocket for something else. You will find that trying will save you money, but if you don't try you will pay whatever they ask. Even if the result is not a monetary savings, you might just get some additional feature or service that you would never have been offered unless you asked. Maybe, the hotel will extend your checkout time for you, or let you use the health club for free.

The quote "Ask and you shall receive," was written in the Bible long ago. After two thousand years this inspirational message still represents a very difficult action for many people to take. You cannot receive anything unless you ask for it first. Do not be afraid to ask. You must overcome this initial fear to gain more in the things you need or want. If you practice these techniques frequently, you will find that that you will become more and more comfortable in asking upfront for what you want.

Do not ever think there is any shame in asking. It is not rude or too forward. It is completely within your rights to find out if there are any alternatives. Remember, the seller is in the business of selling and you are in the business of buying. Think of yourself as a professional buyer.

The minute you picked up this book to learn how to negotiate, you became a professional buyer. As a professional, you are willing to learn about your profession, shopping and buying. This book is a good start. Add to your library other books that will help you buy better. Read other negotiating books—especially those targeted to the seller. The more you learn about what the other side is thinking, the better your chances will be to get the best deal from them.

The alternatives may be limited in small, inexpensive products and services, but there may be some all the same. With larger, higher priced offerings, you can be sure that there are alternatives. You can also bet that the salesperson has been briefed on which alternatives he can release, and when he can do so when he is in a negotiation. He is prepared to offer alternatives; you should be just as prepared to get him to do just that.

Remember, make it a game. Put yourself in the mood to practice the game between buyer and seller. If you are playing baseball, you would not think it strange to want to hit the ball into the bleachers. If you are playing football, you would not think it strange to strategize in a huddle on how you and the team can score a touchdown. Likewise, if you are negotiating to buy a house or a car, it is not at all strange to present an offer lower than the requested price. Similarly, you should view just about every good and service you are offered as negotiable.

The game of negotiating has its rules like any other game and most of them have been delineated in this book. Here's a quick summary of the rules from the buyers side.

1. Research the item you want to buy.

2. Make a list of the potential negotiation points or factors.

3. Ask for the one you really want.

4. Wait for the response quietly. Use silence.

5. If you get what you want stop and buy, if you don't go to 6.

6. Find the reason the seller won't give you what you want.

7. Determine whether to debate those points or bring up another negotiation factor that can be politely discussed.

8. Gain agreement on the lesser need or factor. If this now suits your overall need, buy, otherwise go to 9.

9. Revisit the original requirement. If the seller still will not budge, go back to 7. If he does, buy. If a repetition of points 7 through 9 fail, or you fail to gain any concessions, go to 10.

10. Consider politely backing off the negotiation and trying again elsewhere or at a future time.

The seller is also following a set of rules. He might not have them listed like above, but they are there just the same.

1. Research the items that you sell.

2. Make a list of the potential negotiation points or factors.

3. Ask for the price that you really want.

4. Wait for the response quietly. Use silence.

5. If you get what you want stop and sell it, if you don't go to 6.

6. Find the reason the buyer won't give you what you want.

7. Determine whether to debate those points or bring up another negotiation factor that can be politely discussed.

8. Gain agreement on the lesser need or factor. If this now suits your overall need, sell it, otherwise go to 9.

9. Revisit the original requirement. If the buyer still will not budge, go back to 7. If he does, sell it. If a repetition of points 7 through 9 fail or you fail to gain any concessions, go to 10.

10. Consider a demonstration or money back trial.

11. Do not give up. Keep selling.

Both lists look similar. You will find in practice that many sellers will skip a few points themselves. For example, many sellers will not do the proper research and understand their competition. Think about the buyer who skips that first rule. If he skips the research, he will have less to bargain with. Sellers who skip the first rule also will have less to convince you that their offering is the best.

Let's say that you did not skip your first rule. If you know more about the competition than the seller does, you will gain quickly in the negotiation. If his price is higher than the competitors, you can look to see what he offers ABOVE their offering. If he offers no significant advantage, you now know that he charges too much. You can immediately offer him less. If he will not take it, ask some question that shows you know more about his product. For example, without identifying the competitor, just ask if he offers something that they do that he has not mentioned.

This hint, that you know more about his product, might just be the point you need to make to get the price down. In any event, you get the idea. Knowledge is power. If you know more than the seller, you will be able to use it to your advantage one way or another.

Finding sellers who ignore the basic rules of selling should increase your confidence as a buyer. A seller who fails in playing the basics of the game leaves himself open for the buyer who knows the basics cold. If you know the rules, and you practice, you can win more easily against a seller who does not.

Practice also teaches you the times when you really can and should skip a rule or two. The steps are provided for your education. Once you become proficient, you must learn to recognize that you do not always have to follow each step.

Lists of steps make any process easier to follow. The important trick, though, is to know when to discard the list and move directly to your final goal. For example, many major corporations, when educating their salespeople, will often present their sales process as a series of steps. I was once at a meeting where our salesman presented a compelling offer to our customer for a new product. At the conclusion of his presentation, the customer was obviously impressed and was interested in buying the new product. "What do we need to do?" asked the customer.

Instead of immediately presenting him with a sales contract, the salesman thought about step two in his training and invited the customer to his office for a demonstration. That might have been the right step if the customer was still reluctant to buy, but in this case, the right step would have been, let's say seven, give the customer the contract to sign. By missing his opportunity to immediately close the sale, the rep eventually took months after that initial meeting to win the deal.

Don't make the same mistake as a buyer. You don't need to follow the rules step by step, AS LONG AS, you did your research and you have judged the offering properly. If you find that your first offer is taken, and you are absolutely sure that it is the best you can find, and you are positive that you are getting exactly what you want, go for it.

In most cases, though you should be skeptical when your first offer is accepted quickly. Perhaps, there is a change in the conditions that you did not anticipate.

For example, the house might be at the most attractive price, but did they tell you that they found termite infestation in it last night? You have a right to be skeptical and to patiently take a look to examine that you are try getting what you wanted in the condition that you wanted it in.

But sometimes, blue birds sing your tune. If you find that you are getting your need fulfilled do not feel compelled to negotiate further. For example, if the seller is truly in a distressed position, you might gain an extra dollar by pushing the negotiation to the extreme, but you might also anger or annoy the seller.

Remember to focus on winning twice. If you are satisfied with the offer, do not be afraid to leave something on the table for the seller. You will be happy and he will be happy that you did not take advantage of him. If you are the type of person who does not find that a personally rewarding, altruistic situation, you can still take solace in the fact that you may have to deal with him again. Make friends not enemies.

Your practice in small negotiations will build your confidence to handle the bigger ones. Soon your skills will become automatic. You will intuitively seek out the best deal. You will know you have made it when the sellers begin to compliment you on your negotiation skill.

I still remember a car dealer who was in the act of complimenting my negotiation skills when he realized that I had saved even more than he had intended to offer. He was about to sign the sales contract when he realized that I managed to even reduce my down payment on the purchase to zero. With his pen hovering above the contract, he said that he thought I was going to put some money down. I agreed I did say that, but only when we began talking a few weeks earlier. I told him that we had gotten beyond that point last week. I then shut my mouth.

He smiled and then signed the contract. Like two evenly matched gamesmen, he could live with my success on the price and I could live with his sale of the car. Practice your negotiation skills and you can not only get what you want but earn the respect of the professionals.

Good luck and keep negotiating!

0-595-28300-4